REVIEWER PRAISE OF BOOKS BY DOUGLAS GRAY

Making Money in Real Estate

"Gray delivers the goods. It is all-Canadian, and not a retread book full of tips that are worthless north of the U.S. border. It's chock-full of practical streetsmart strategies and advice, pitfalls to avoid, samples, what-to-look-out for, checklists and information."
—*Business in Vancouver*

"...provides consumer insights into securing the best deal and avoiding the pitfalls...Gray's legal background has given him valuable insights."
—*The Edmonton Journal*

"Outstanding...peppered with practical no-nonsense tips...invaluable information throughout."
—*Calgary Herald*

The Complete Canadian Small Business Guide
(with Diana Gray)

"This guide is truly a gold mine...an admirable job...taps into the author's expertise."
—*Profit Magazine*

"Excellent...geared especially to Canadians, unlike most small business guides"
—*Financial Times*

"The most informative and comprehensive guide on this subject matter."
—*The Toronto Star*

Home Inc.: The Canadian Home-Based Business Guide

"Should be required reading for all potential home-basers... authoritative, current and comprehensive."
—*The Edmonton Journal*

"An absolute necessity for your bookshelf...crammed with useful information."
—*Victoria Times-Colonist*

The Complete Canadian Franchise Guide
(with Norm Friend)

"Down to earth, comprehensive, easy to read and packed with practical information. A superb guide to buying a franchise. Invaluable samples and checklists. Highly recommended."
—Terry and Fran Banting, *Franchisees*

The Canadian Snowbird Guide

"...an invaluable guide to worry-free part-time living in the U.S....by one of Canada's bestselling authors of business and personal finance books..."
—*The Globe and Mail*

"...Gray has written a reference book, thoughtful and complete, and prepared with the authoritative research skills and knowledge of a fastidious solicitor...as practical as a sunhat on a Tampa afternoon, and that alone warrants it a place on every southbound RV's bookshelf."
—*Quill & Quire*

The Canadian Guide to Will and Estate Planning
(with John Budd)

"...An informative, practical guide...the authors...cover all the bases."
—*The National Post*

"...A bargain for its price, it should be part of every family's library."
—*The Globe and Mail*

101
STREETSMART
CONDO
BUYING TIPS
FOR CANADIANS

Other Books by the Author

Real Estate

Making Money in Real Estate: The Canadian Guide to Profitable Investment in Residential Property

101 Streetsmart Condo Buying Tips for Canadians

Mortgages Made Easy: The All-Canadian Guide to Home Financing

Real Estate Investing for Canadians for Dummies (with Peter Mitham)

Canadian Home Buying Made Easy

Condo Buying Made Easy: The Canadian Guide to Apartment and Townhouse Condos, Co-ops and Timeshares

Mortgage Payment Tables Made Easy

Small Business

Start and Run a Profitable Consulting Business

Start a Profitable Business Using Your Computer

Have You Got What It Takes? The Entrepreneur's Complete Self-Assessment Guide

Marketing Your Product (with Donald Cyr)

The Complete Canadian Small Business Guide (with Diana Gray)

Home, Inc.: The Canadian Home-Based Business Guide (with Diana Gray)

Raising Money: The Canadian Guide to Successful Business Financing (with Brian Nattrass)

The Complete Canadian Franchise Guide (with Norm Friend)

So You Want to Buy a Franchise? (with Norm Friend)

Be Your Own Boss: The Ultimate Guide to Buying a Small Business or Franchise in Canada (with Norm Friend)

The Canadian Small Business Legal Guide

Personal Finance/Retirement Planning

The Canadian Snowbird Guide: Everything You Need to Know about Living Part-time in the U.S.A. and Mexico

The Canadian Guide to Will and Estate Planning (with John Budd)

Risk-Free Retirement: The Complete Canadian Planning Guide (with Tom Delaney, Graham Cunningham, Les Solomon and Dr. Des Dwyer)

Software Programs

Making Money in Real Estate (Jointly developed by Douglas Gray and Phoenix Accrual Corporation)

101
STREETSMART
CONDO
BUYING TIPS
FOR CANADIANS

How to Avoid the Pitfalls, Make the Right Decisions,
Save Money, Protect Your Investment,
and Find Peace of Mind

By

DOUGLAS GRAY

John Wiley & Sons Canada, Ltd.

Library and Archives Canada Cataloguing in Publication Data

Gray, Douglas A
    101 streetsmart condo buying tips for Canadians / Douglas A. Gray.

ISBN-13 978-0-470-83812-9
ISBN-10 0-470-83812-4

    1. Condominiums—Purchasing—Canada. 2. House buying—Canada. I. Title. II. Title: One hundred one streetsmart condo buying tips for Canadians.

HD7287.67.C3G735 2006   643'.12   C2006-901424-8

Production Credits:
Cover design: Ian Koo
Interior text design: Natalia Burobina
Printer: Tri-Graphic Printing Limited

John Wiley & Sons Canada, Ltd.
6045 Freemont Blvd., Mississauga, Ontario L5R 4J3

Printed in Canada

1 2 3 4 5 TRI 10 09 08 07 06

Contents

Acknowledgements

I am grateful for the kind assistance given me by many parties, including the Canada and Mortgage Housing Corporation, the Canadian Real Estate Association, Genworth Financial Canada, and Royal LePage.

I would like to thank Nicole Langlois for the superb quality of editing that she has demonstrated throughout. Her insights, creative suggestions, and positive attitude made the editorial experience a most pleasurable one.

I would like to thank the staff of John Wiley & Sons Canada for their support, professionalism, and insightful feedback.

Last but not least, I would like to express my appreciation to Don Loney, Executive Editor of John Wiley & Sons Canada, for his patience and encouragement in the development of this book. I have had the pleasure of knowing Don for over 15 years. I have indeed been fortunate to work with such a consummate professional in the publishing business.

Introduction

Buying a condominium can be a confusing process. Many people do not even know what a condominium is, or the legal structure and responsibilities, or unique community lifestyle dynamics that are involved in owning one.

A book was therefore needed that explained, step by step, what a Canadian buyer or owner of a condominium needs to consider in order to make informed and prudent choices. By providing 101 key tips you need to know, this guide is designed to fulfill that need.

The legal, financial, and practical issues involved in buying, owning, and selling a condominium are discussed in detail. You will see the 101 tips broken down into six main categories.

In addition, there is helpful information in the appendix. These include key websites for further information, checklists, and a glossary to help you comprehend the terminology used in this book. Terminology can differ, depending on the province; however, the basic concepts are the same. You'll find these differences explained in both the text and the glossary.

The content of this book is based on my professional experience as a real estate and business lawyer, my personal experience living in a townhouse condominium for many years and being chairman of the legal committee of the condo council/board, and my business experience as an investor in residential real estate, including condominiums. This book is also based on extensive interviews with others in the condominium industry—lawyers, realtors, developers, management companies, insurance and mortgage brokers, bankers and condominium owners, investors, and renters.

I hope you enjoy this book, and find the information helpful and encouraging. If you would like to provide some feedback, learn more about upcoming seminars, or add your name to a list for a free e-mail newsletter, please refer to the Reader Feedback section at the back of the book, or go to www.homebuyer.ca.

Note from the publisher: For the sake of simplicity, only the masculine form of the personal pronoun has been employed throughout the book in cases where the gender of its antecedent is unknown.

CHAPTER 1

Is a Condomonium the Right Lifestyle Choice for Me?

Several areas will be covered in this chapter, including an overview of what a condominium is, community living, types of condos, pitfalls to avoid when purchasing a condo, and the advantages and disadvantages of condominium ownership.

Tip #1: Condo Course 101

Condominiums are a popular form of shared home ownership in Canada. On average, 20 to 25% of housing in major Canadian cities are condominium apartments or townhouses. New condo developments are driving sales in many urban communities. Condominiums in resort areas are also very popular.

The word *condominium* refers to a specific form of shared legal ownership. Although this book concentrates primarily on residential condominiums, there are other types, including resort and commercial.

The word *condominium* does not imply a specific structural form, but a legal form. Condominiums (called co-proprietorships in Quebec) may be detached, semi-detached, row houses, stack townhouses, duplexes, or apartments. They can even be building lots, subdivisions, or mobile home parks. Whatever the style, a residential unit is specified and is owned outright by the individual owner in fee simple, which means that you own the title to the property outright; it is not on leased property. The rest of the property, including land, which is called the *common elements* (or *common property*) in most provinces, is owned in common with the other owners. That is, an individual owner would own a fractional share of the common elements in the development. If there are 50 condominium owners, then each individual owner would own 1/50 as tenants-in-common of the common elements. The legislation of each province varies, but it is always designed to provide the legal and structural framework for the efficient management and administration of each condominium project. Once the project documents are registered, the project is brought into legal being as a form of tenure.

The part of the condominium that you will own outright is referred to as the *unit* in most provinces. You will have full and clear title to this unit when you purchase it, which will be legally registered in your name in the land registry office in your province. The precise description of the common elements, and exactly what you own as part of your unit, may differ from development to development, but in any event it will be provided for in the documents prepared and registered for each condominium.

Common elements generally include walkways, driveways, lawns and gardens, lobbies, elevators, parking areas, recreational facilities, storage areas, laundry rooms, stairways, plumbing, electrical systems and portions of walls, ceilings and floors, and other items. Parts of the common elements may be designated for the exclusive use of one or more of the individual unit owners, in which case these are called *limited common elements* (or *limited common property*). Examples would include parking spaces, roof gardens, balconies, storage lockers, and front and back yards.

Condominiums can be built on freehold or leasehold properties. (These definitions are covered in chapter 5.) A condominium can also be in a stratified format, where a legal description for the unit is allocated in a vertical dimension. In other words, if you live in a condominium apartment on the 30th floor, there is a precise legal description in the land registry office for the specific unit in the complex. Another form is a bare land condominium. In this example, it would be similar to a building lot subdivision with individual units owned by the unit holders, although the units would appear as detached homes. The rest of the land would be considered common elements.

A condominium development is administered by various legal structures set out in provincial legislation. (This is covered in chapter 2.)

There are many reasons why the condominium concept has been economically very attractive for purchasers: better land utilization, price competitiveness, built-in amenities, and convenient locations and designs. There is also a wide price range, from $50,000 to well over a million dollars, depending on the features, level of luxury, and location.

Large segments of the market find the multi-family residential development concept an attractive alternative for their lifestyles, due to the low maintenance required and the opportunity for equity appreciation. Condominium ownership appeals to active young singles, couples without children, couples with children, and pre-retirement and retired couples or singles. Many developments are geared specifically to these segments or to a mixture of these segments.

The concept of condominium living is not right for everyone, as it involves not only individual ownership in the unit and shared ownership in other property, but also adherence to rules and regulations, and shared ruler-ship.

Tip #2: Understanding the Types of Condos in the Market

There are numerous types of condominium formats for residential, recreational, resort, and commercial purposes. Here is an overview of the most common options.

Residential Condominiums

Residential condominiums can be found in either a metropolitan or suburban setting. In a metropolitan setting the most common formats are:

- a modern high-rise apartment building.
- a new three-to-five-storey mid-rise building.
- a converted older building that formerly consisted of rental apartments.
- a building where the street-level floor is owned jointly by the condominium corporation members (the unit owners) and which is rented out to retailers to help offset the common maintenance fees of the residential condominiums in the rest of the building.
- same format as the previous example, except that the retail spaces are sold as condominiums.

Suburban condominiums tend to be of a different format and are most often found in the form of:

- cluster housing consisting of multi-unit structures, using housing of two to four units apiece, each with its own private entranceway.

- townhouse-type single-family homes distributed in rows.
- garden apartments consisting of a group of apartment buildings surrounding a common green, frequently with each of the floors held by separate condominium owners.
- a series of detached single-family homes in a subdivision format, all utilizing the same land and parking areas.
- duplexes, triplexes, or fourplexes.

The suburban condominium format tends to make maximum use of the land while creating attractive views, private driveways, and common recreational facilities such as swimming pools, tennis courts, saunas, playgrounds, etc. Many residential condominium developments, with the conveniences and amenities being offered, have created a complete lifestyle experience. The purpose of these separate developments—restaurants, shopping centres, recreational and entertainment facilities, and care facilities for older people—is to make the condominium community a very distinct and self-contained environment and community for many people.

Recreational Condos

Recreational condominiums can take various forms, including mobile home parks where the "pad," with utility hookups, is owned in fee simple by the individual owner, with a share in the common elements of the rest of the park. Alternatively, it could be in a leasehold format. Another option is to create bare land condominiums in rural, wilderness, or waterfront areas. In these examples an owner could build a cabin with fee simple ownership to the land underneath and a partial interest in the common elements. The common elements could include a marina, beach, farm, or forest. Common recreational facilities could include a playground or community centre, and assets could include boats or even farm animals.

Resort Condos

The development in resort areas is extensive and condominiums are frequently built on lakeshores, sea coasts, or island resorts, or in ski country. There are two main types of resort condominiums: those developed for warmer climates and those developed for winter climates.

The warmer-climate type is generally built around a common recreational facility that can be enjoyed throughout the year by the owners, one that includes such facilities as a seashore, lake, marina, or golf course. The buildings tend to range from high-rise apartments to cluster housing.

Winter resort areas tend to be built near popular ski resort developments. Many tend to provide recreational facilities for the summer season as well, such as golf courses, tennis courts, and swimming pools, making it a year-round resort. The buildings tend to be in the form of cluster housing, modular housing, attached townhouses, or bare land detached homes.

People who purchase a recreational or resort condominium tend to:

- Own it outright and use it throughout the year for lifestyle enjoyment
- Own it outright and rent it when not in use by using the condominium corporation or property management company as an agent, using a real estate agent, or renting it independently and directly.
- Own a portion of the condominium and use it for personal use and/or rentals, with the time available commensurate with the percentage equity ownership.

Commercial/Industrial Condos

Ownership of a commercial or an industrial condominium is similar in concept to ownership of a residential one. There are various reasons why condominiums for commercial purposes are an attractive alternative to renting space, buying land with a building on it, or buying land and building on it. Some of the benefits include:

- Tax advantages for an owner-occupier of his or her own business premises including depreciation, expense deductions for mortgage interest, etc.
- Placing a limit on monthly costs by carefully regulating costs through the condominium corporation policies.
- Avoiding rent increases.

- Shared contribution of costs for features such as maintenance, security, common facilities, and advertising.

- Appreciation in value of the condominium over time.

- Right to participate in the decision-making relating to the condominium development.

- Opportunity to be assured of remaining in a unique location that is commercially attractive.

- Removal of the financial risk of owning an entire building.

- Providing an alternative if there is a lack of financial capability or desire to own the whole building.

Types of Commercial/Industrial Condos

The three main types of commercial-use condominiums are office buildings, professional buildings, and industrial parks.

Office Buildings

In Canada, commercial condos are a popular concept in many major cities and involve a cross-section of retail and service businesses operating through the condominium structure.

Professional Buildings

A familiar form of office use is the dental or medical condominium, where each dentist or doctor owns a suite. The nature of a dental or medical office is often such that it does not expand in size as other businesses do. Another advantage for the professional is the possibility of sharing reception areas, central telephone answering, accounting areas, and expensive equipment. It is fairly common in this type of building to sell or lease the street-level condominiums to retail outlets such as pharmacies, laboratory or x-ray service groups, magazine stands, restaurants, etc. Lawyers also own offices in condominium buildings and take the same approach as dentists and doctors in terms of shared office space, reception area, library area, word processing, etc.

Industrial Parks

Industrial parks established on a bare land condominium format are a popular development. They can be advantageous due to the fact that the business can have the individual unit for its industrial or manufacturing needs but can share in the common elements such as docks, loading areas, rail sidings, etc.

Tip #3: Advantages to Look for in a Condo Community Lifestyle

In any situation of shared ownership and community living, there are advantages and disadvantages. Here are the advantages:

- Protection from arbitrary rent increases.
- Ready availability of financing as a single-family home.
- Range of prices, locations, types of structures, sizes, and architectural features available.
- Availability of amenities such as swimming pool, tennis courts, health clubs, community centre, saunas, hot tubs, exercise rooms, sun decks, etc.
- Benefits of home ownership in terms of participation in the real estate market and potential growth in equity.
- Individual ownership of living units with security of tenure and permanence of occupancy.
- Pride in home ownership.
- Enables people of moderate and middle-income levels to own their own home. Condominiums are often considerably cheaper than single-family homes because of more efficient use of land and economy of scale.
- Freedom to decorate interior of unit to suit personal tastes.
- Enhanced security.
- Elimination of many of the problems of upkeep and maintenance often associated with home ownership, since maintenance is usually the responsibility of a professional agency or manager.

- Investment opportunity for profit if selected carefully.

- Good transitional type of home between rental apartments and single-family houses for growing families or singles or couples; conversely, good transition for downsizing "empty nesters" who wish to give up their larger family house.

- Reduction of costs due to responsibilities for repair and maintenance being shared in many cases, as some owners will contribute considerable volunteer work.

- Enhancement of social activities and sense of community by relative permanence of residents.

- Elected council that is responsible for many business and management decisions.

- Participation of owners in the operation of the development, which involves playing a role in budget-setting and approval, decision-making, determination of rules and bylaws, and other matters affecting the democratic operation of the condominium community.

Tip #4: Disadvantages to Think About in a Condo Community Lifestyle

A condominium lifestyle is not for everyone. Here are some of the drawbacks that might influence your decision about buying a condo:

- Real estate appreciation is generally not as high as for a single-family house, simply because it is the land that appreciates in value in a single-family house, and the flexibility of use of that land. However, there are many exceptions to this general rule in metropolitan settings.

- It may be difficult to accurately assess the quality of construction of the project.

- Unacceptable loss of freedom may be experienced through restrictions contained in the rules and bylaws. For example, there may be restrictions on the right to rent, restrictions on pets, etc.

- People live closer together, thereby potentially creating problems from time to time. The most common problem areas are the "five p's": pets, parking, personalities, parties, and people.

- Flexibility may be affected if circumstances require that the condominium be sold in a limited time, as condominiums generally sell more slowly than single-family houses.

- Money is tied up in the condominium ownership, which may affect immediate liquidity needs in certain circumstances.

- One could be paying for maintenance and operation of amenities that one has no desire or intention to use (e.g., swimming pool or recreational centre).

- Management of the condominium council is by volunteers, who may or may not have the appropriate abilities, skills, and personality.

- There is possible apathy of owners, so that it is always the same people who are able and wiling to serve on council.

- Some elected councils behave in an autocratic fashion.

- Mix between living in a single-family house and in a landlord–tenant relationship could cause conflict and frustration depending on people's needs, expectations, and past housing experiences.

The major factors that are driving the popularity of condominiums are affordability and location—proximity to downtown cores or rapid transit. Older couples who are downsizing or young couples who are about to make their first purchase are finding that condos are right for them, but for different reasons.

Tip #5: The Benefits of Buying a Condo as an Investment

The first-time real estate investor could find buying a condominium unit, and renting it out, an attractive option for several reasons. If you are considering investing in a condominium, it is important to consider the advantages and disadvantages of the different types of condominiums, for example, apartment, conversion, or townhouse. You must ascertain whether rental units are permitted in a development and you should know the mix of tenants and owner/occupiers.

Here are some of the benefits of condo investment:

- Condominiums generally appreciate in value at a rate which is almost consistently higher than the inflation rate.

- Finding an occupant for a condominium apartment is relatively easy in many major Canadian cities because of low vacancy rates.

- There is an increasing demand for the condominium lifestyle and the luxury and convenience that it provides.

- Because a minimal amount of upkeep is involved, the economic benefits are more attractive for the first-time investor.

- There is the convenience of having many of the management and maintenance problems taken care of by the condominium corporation, and the professional management company, if any.

- Facilities such as tennis courts and swimming pools are maintained by the condominium corporation, thereby freeing the new investor from the responsibilities of upkeep.

- The owner is protected by provincial condominium legislation, by the original project documents, and by the bylaws and rules and regulations of the condominium corporation. For example, many condominiums do not allow pets in the building because of the potential wear and tear on the apartment. This type of rule protects and benefits the investor.

If you are looking for higher appreciation (resale value), the purchase of the least expensive unit in a luxury condominium/townhouse complex generally offers a more financially attractive return than the purchase of the largest unit in a modestly priced development, assuming the price is the same. A townhouse condominium generally appreciates faster than an apartment condominium. Your research will provide you with the necessary background statistics in your market interest area.

CHAPTER 2

A Crash Course in How a Condominium Is Run and Managed—and What That Can Mean for an Owner

There are two main governing structures: the condominium corporation (referred to as the strata corporation in British Columbia and as the co-proprietors in Quebec) and the condominium council (referred to as the strata council in British Columbia). All condo owners automatically become voting members of the condominium corporation. Normally, only one vote is given for each unit, regardless of the unit size or the number of owners of that unit.

The operation and management of a condominium development is similar to that of a company. In a company, those who own part of the company are shareholders, and collectively they control the company. Major decisions are voted on at the annual general meeting, and at the same meeting the board of directors is elected to run the day-by-day operations of the company on the shareholders' behalf. The condominium corporation performs a role similar to that of the shareholders in a company, while the condo council operates much like a board of directors.

As you can see, there are a lot of controlling elements built into the condominium community structure in order to maintain consistency, continuity, and control for the betterment of all the members of the development. In addition to federal, provincial, and municipal government laws and regulations that impact on the development, there is in effect a fourth level of government. In many ways a condominium development may be similar to a self-contained and self-governed community. Naturally, the bureaucratic nature and extent of this fourth level of government depends on its size, membership, and history.

The tips in this chapter address the common powers and duties of a condominium corporation and a condominium council. The exact duties and responsibilities can vary from province to province depending on the legislation and the original project documents or bylaws. As mentioned, terminology can differ in each province, but the concepts are similar.

Tip #6: Read the Act

The Condominium Act of each province (under various names) is the basic legislative document that sets out the procedural requirements for the operation of condominiums. This is supplemented by other legal documents that are specialized for each development such as the project document, bylaws, and rules and regulations. If you are serious about buying a condo, it is imperative that you obtain copies of these documents and others, as well as of the condominium legislation, before you finalize your purchase. In most cases, people don't review this material thoroughly and understand it before purchasing. By the time you are through this book, you will better appreciate the need to be aware of the contents of the laws that will regulate you. A copy of the Act for your province can be obtained from your provincial government. Refer to the Appendix under Helpful Websites for a listing of the appropriate government departments to contact.

Tip #7: Know the Powers of the Council

Although there can be differences in provincial legislation, there are common powers and duties that condo boards and council members have across the country. Here is an overview. Your lawyer can give you specific advice for your province and municipality.

The condominium council has the power to:

- Meet for the conduct of business, and adjourn and otherwise regulate its meetings as it thinks fit. It shall meet when any member gives the other members not less than seven days' notice of a meeting proposed by him, specifying the reason for calling the meeting, unless the other members agree to waive the notice.

- Employ for, and on behalf of the condominium corporation, agents and employees as it thinks proper for the control, management, and administration of the common property, common facilities, or other assets of the corporation, and the exercise and performance of the powers and duties of the corporation.

- Delegate to one or more of its members, or to a member or committee of members of the condominium corporation, or to its manager, those of its powers and duties it thinks proper, and at any time revoke such a delegation.

The council must keep, in one location, or in the possession of one person, and shall make available on request to an owner or a person authorized by him:

- a copy of the Condominium Act and changes in the bylaws
- a copy of special or unanimous resolutions
- a copy of all the legal agreements to which the corporation is a party, including management contracts, insurance policies, insurance trustee agreements, deeds, agreements for sale, leases, licenses, easements, or rights of way
- a register of the members of the council
- a register of unit owners, setting out the unit number, the name of the owner, the unit entitlement, the name and address of any mortgagee who has notified the condominium corporation, the name of any tenant or lessee, and a notation of any assignment by the owner to the lessee
- the annual budget for each year
- minutes of all general meetings and of all council meetings.

The council must:

- keep minutes of its proceedings
- cause minutes to be kept of general meetings
- cause proper books of account to be kept in respect of all sums of money received and expended by it, and the matters in respect of which receipt and expenditure take place
- prepare proper accounts relating to all money of the corporation, and the income and expenditure of it, for each annual general meeting
- on application of an owner or mortgagee, or a person authorized in writing by him, make the books of account available for inspection at all reasonable times.

Tip #8: Who Minds the Farm?

Because there are many duties which volunteer members of the condominium council do not have the time, skill, or inclination to fulfill, such as maintenance, repair, and the administration of routine matters, a management company is frequently hired under contract with the condominium corporation to deal with those tasks. Other procedures can also be set up to deal with routine matters.

The Condominium Act in most provinces permits the council to employ a professional property management company to carry out these daily functions. The management company's authority and responsibility are limited to matters affecting the security and maintenance of the common elements, and the assets and facilities of the condominium corporation. This limitation is to ensure that the management company does not take over the decision-making role of the council.

The initial decision regarding management is usually made by the owner/developer prior to any deal. The terms of the management contract, if any, and the relationship between the developer and the property manager, are required to be included in the original project documents that are filed in the land registry. The decision will be largely determined by the size of the project. Some larger developers have internal divisions which carry out the property management function. Under most Condominium Acts, the council can terminate the management contract established by the owner/developer within a certain period after the development is completed and registered, or at the time that a certain percentage of the units are sold.

There are essentially three forms of condominium management: self-management, resident management, and professional management. A combination of these options may also be employed.

Self-management

In smaller condominium developments, it is often more practical for the owners to be responsible for the management of the development directly. For example, in a condominium duplex or development of up to approximately 15 units, this self-management alternative could be attractive. Another example would be a bare land condominium corporation with detached houses, and which has minimal common elements and facilities to maintain.

It is not necessary in a self-management situation that the owners themselves clean the grounds, cut the grass, do the gardening, and sweep the driveways. It does mean, though, that the owners, or a representative of the owners, would have to be directly involved in supervising the performance of these types of services. Frequently the jobs are done by volunteers, part-time or full-time employees, contracting firms, or combinations of this type of help. For the sake of continuity and accurate delegation of responsibilities, it is important that someone on council be responsible for communicating with those who are providing the services.

In addition to communicating with the staff, some form of supervision will have to be put into place to monitor such services as maintenance of the pool, grounds, and elevators, painting, garbage removal, and accounting and typing functions. Various federal and provincial government responsibilities relating to employees will also have to be considered, such as unemployment insurance, income tax deductions from employees' wages, and Workers' Compensation Board contributions. If the council negotiates with a contractor to provide services, then deductions do not have to be taken off in the same fashion as with employees, because the contractor would be signing a written agreement to the effect that he will hire and pay his own employees. In that event, the council would simply pay the negotiated contract fee for services rendered by the contractor.

Another reason for self-management is that a condominium development may be outside the metropolitan area, making it difficult to obtain the services of a professional property management company.

Resident Management

In this situation, the condominium corporation employs one or more people directly to perform the daily management requirements. These people would normally operate out of an office in the development and would be paid a full-time or part-time salary. Because the manager would be an employee of the condominium corporation, he would in effect be an employee of all the owners; it is therefore important to be very careful in selecting the manager, in order to maintain harmony with the members. Generally only large condominium developments can financially justify employing a full-time resident manager.

Professional Management

Many condominium corporations use a professional management company to some extent. These companies tend to be experienced at condominium management, and have many systems and procedures for efficient operation of their support function. This would include computerized accounting procedures and management systems, experienced staff, access to suppliers who can provide bulk-buying discounts and goods service, and careful selection of competent tradespeople. One of the key benefits of using a professional management company is that due to the periodic turnover of council members, such a company will provide the continuity of management that ensures a consistent level of quality in the condominium development. The responsibility of the condominium council would be one of providing instructions to the management company and monitoring the company's performance.

Tip #9: Can You Live with Your Obligations as a Condo Owner?

A condominium owner has certain legal duties and responsibilities arising out of the owning of a condominium and being a member of a condominium corporation. Although the duties and responsibilities can vary from development to development and from province to province, most of the legal requirements cover the same general topic areas and are outlined in the bylaws and the rules and regulations. The following are examples of typical bylaws relating to the responsibilities of the condominium owner.

The owner must:

- Permit the condominium corporation and its agents, at all reasonable times on notice, except in case of emergency when no notice is required, to enter his unit for the purpose of inspecting, repairing, and maintaining pipes, wires, cables, ducts, or other common assets of the condominium corporation within the unit.

- Promptly carry out all work that may be ordered by any competent public or local authority in respect of unit other than work for the benefit of the building generally, and pay all rates, taxes, charges, and assessments that may be payable in respect of his unit.

- Repair and maintain his unit, including windows and doors, and areas allocated to his exclusive use, and keep them in a good state of repair.

- Use and enjoy the common elements, common facilities, or other assets of the condominium corporation in a manner that will not unreasonably interfere with their use and enjoyment by other owners, their families, or visitors.

- Not use his unit, or permit it to be used, for a purpose that will cause a nuisance or hazard to any occupier of a unit, whether an owner or not.

- Notify the condominium corporation promptly on any change of ownership or of any mortgage or other dealing in connection with his unit.

- Comply strictly with the bylaws of the condominium corporation, and with the rules and regulations as adopted from time to time.

- Receive the written permission of the condominium council before undertaking alterations to the exterior or structure of the unit.

- Pay his share of the common expenses established by the condominium corporation, including any special assessments.

- Pay his share of any judgment registered against the common elements. *Note:* This liability arises because the unit owner owns a share of the common elements as a tenant in common. For this reason owners should be aware of the extent of liability insurance arranged by the condominium corporation.

Tip #10: Know Your Rights Before You Buy—You Could be Surprised

Your rights as a condo owner are defined by the condominium legislation of your province, and the bylaws, rules, and regulations of the condominium project that you are buying into. Also, if there have been court cases brought for or against condo owners in your province, there could be case law that further defines your rights. If you are entitled to rent your condo, your rights as a landlord would be defined by the landlord/tenant legislation of your province, and by any tenancy agreement that you sign.

Issues that are important to you need to be clarified before you buy your condo, for example, whether you can keep a pet, rent your condo, or operate a home business. Age restrictions may also be in place, since some communities do not allow children to reside there. After you do your due diligence by obtaining all the documents about the condo to review in advance, you should speak to a lawyer who practises in the area of condo law to get specific feedback.

Tip #11: The McCoys vs. the Hatfields

In the condominium community, there is always a possibility of having a problem or a dispute that may not be able to be resolved quickly and easily. It is
important to know your rights and options in that event.

Problems tend to fall into the following general categories:

The Five P's: Pets, Parking, Parties, People, Personalities

The five p's tend to be the most common areas of annoyance. Common complaints are: *Pets* are noisy, roaming, scaring children, or fouling the common
property. *Parking spaces* are being used by members or guests in a consistently
selfish and irresponsible fashion. *People* and *parties* are too loud for too long
at too-late hours. *Personalities* may become a problem because of the close
proximity of the community environment; some owners get annoyed by people using or abusing the common elements, and some people have a tendency
to irritate others by virtue of their attitude, arrogance, indifference, or lack of
courtesy.

Decisions of the Condominium Corporation or Council that Can Affect You

You may dispute orders of council in a number of areas. Here are some examples: you believe that the conduct of the corporation or council is oppressive
and unfairly prejudicial to your rights; you believe that a decision relating to a
special assessment was unnecessary and irresponsible; you were fined for alleg-
edly breaching the bylaws or rules and regulations, and you believe the fine was
unfair and unwarranted.

Tip #12: When in Dispute . . .

The means for the resolution of disputes, in ascending order of complexity, are
negotiation, council involvement, mediation, arbitration, and litigation.

Negotiation

It is always best to attempt to resolve the dispute by discussing the matter directly with the person concerned. That may be all that is necessary to resolve the problem. It is worthwhile to at least attempt that first step.

Council Involvement

If the first step is not successful, you may wish to contact the condominium council and make a complaint to them in writing, outlining your dispute. If the conduct of another owner has contravened the bylaws or rules and regulations, it would be helpful to draw those points to the attention of the council. The council has the authority in most cases to deal with infringements of the bylaws or rules and regulations, or can seek legal advice.

Mediation

This option may be built into the condo corporation's bylaws. It would generally involve a professional mediator or condominium lawyer performing the role of attempting to facilitate a mutually agreeable resolution. The purpose is to hear both sides of the issue and try to come to some pragmatic and constructive resolution that is a workable compromise. Mediation is non-binding.

Arbitration

If your attempts to have a dispute resolved through using the condominium council have not been successful, you may wish to consider arbitration. Condominium legislation of most provinces sets out the procedures for the arbitration process. Normally, the process is not available if litigation has commenced. Matters that may require arbitration include disputes about contributions to common expenses; fines for breach of bylaws or rules and regulations; damages to common elements, common facilities, and other assets of the condominium corporation; and decisions of the council or the corporation.

The parties should agree on a single arbitrator, but if that is not possible, each party selects its own arbitrator and the two arbitrators select a third who acts as chair. Unless the parties otherwise agree, the arbitrator is normally a professional arbitrator. The arbitrators may accept evidence under oath and may make whatever decision they consider just and equitable. The arbitrator's decision is entered into court as if it were an order of the court. The process just described is a common procedure set out in many provincial condominium laws, although the procedures may vary from province to province.

A list of arbitrators is available upon request from most professional condominium management companies.

Litigation

If all else fails, you have rights in common law, as well as under most provincial condominium legislation, to commence action in court. You can proceed against a condominium corporation or council to rectify what you believe is a failure to meet their obligations under the Condominium Act or bylaws, or because you feel that actions toward you have been oppressive. The court can make any order it considers appropriate depending on the circumstances.

The difficulty in the litigation process, of course, is the fact that it can be very expensive, stressful, uncertain, and lengthy. If you have a problem that you are concerned about and want to decide whether you should go the arbitration or the litigation route, you should seek a legal opinion from a lawyer who specializes in condominium law. Ideally it would be helpful to obtain a second opinion from another lawyer who specializes in condominium law in order to satisfy yourself that the advice you are getting and intend to rely on is consistent. (How to select a lawyer is covered in chapter 5.)

Tip #13: The Cost of Membership: Part 1

As an owner of a condo, you must be prepared to pay costs that reflect belonging to a community. You must factor these in to your purchase decision. As an owner of a condominium unit, there are ongoing monthly or annual expenses and potential expenses that you have to plan for. The most common expenses are as follows:

Mortgage Payments

Unless you paid cash for your unit, you will be making monthly payments for principal, interest, and probably taxes. Details on financing a condominium by obtaining a mortgage are covered in chapter 3.

Property Taxes

Each individual condominium unit is assessed by the municipality and has to make an annual payment for the property taxes. If you have a mortgage, the lender may or may not have required you to include extra monthly payments along with your mortgage. These are held in a property tax account so that the lender can pay your municipal property taxes annually. If you do not have a mortgage, you will have to pay property tax separately. The common elements have a property tax as well, but that tax is covered in your monthly maintenance payments.

Maintenance Payments

Maintenance payments or "assessments for common expenses" cover all the operating costs of the common elements and are adjusted accordingly for any increase or decrease in expenses. You are responsible for a portion of the development's total operating cost. The formula for determining your portion will be discussed shortly. The payments for common expenses are made directly to the condominium corporation and generally cover the following items:

Maintenance and Repair of Common Property

This includes costs for maintenance, landscaping, building repairs, recreational facilities, equipment, and other expenses.

Operating and Service Costs

These include expenses relating to garbage removal, heat, electricity, and municipal water supply.

Contingency Reserve Fund

This is a fund for unforeseen problems and expenses. For example, unexpectedly the roof needs repair/replacement or the heating/cooling system breaks down. This fund is for expenses that have not been included in the annual budgeted expense calculations for the common property and other assets of the condominium corporation. Owners contribute monthly to this fund, on the basis of a portion of the monthly maintenance fee. The condominium legislation in most provinces requires a minimum amount to be contributed by owners to the contingency reserve fund (e.g., 10% of the annual budget). If you are buying an older condominium, you should check to see what percentage of the monthly payments is being allocated toward this fund, as there is a higher risk of needing to use the fund in older buildings than in new developments. In older buildings, the fund should likely be 25% or more, depending on the circumstances.

In most cases you are not entitled to a refund of your contribution to the reserve fund when you sell your unit, or have it calculated on the purchase and sale statement of adjustments.

Management Costs

These are the costs associated with hiring private individuals or professional management firms to administer all or part of the daily functions of the condominium development.

Condo Corporation Insurance

Condominium legislation requires that the development carry sufficient fire and related insurance to replace the common property in the event of fire or other damage. Condominium corporations generally obtain further insurance to cover other payables and liabilities. The insurance does not cover the damage done to the interior of an individual unit. The cost of condo insurance for the corporation is included in your monthly maintenance fees.

Special Assessment

There may be situations in which 75% or more of the condominium members wish to raise funds for special purposes. These funds would not be able to come from the contingency reserve fund or from the regular monthly assessments. For example, there could be an interest in building a swimming pool or tennis courts, or it may be necessary to cover costs of repairs beyond the contingency reserve fund. Once the decision is made to assess members, you cannot refuse to pay the special assessment if it has been properly approved, even though you might not agree with its purpose.

Lease Payments

If you have a leasehold condominium, you will be required to make monthly lease payments in addition to many of the other costs outlined in this section.

Tip #14: The Cost of Membership: Part 2

Condominium Owner Insurance

As mentioned earlier, the insurance on the building that is covered by the condominium development *does not* include the interior of your unit. Therefore, you will need to get separate insurance to cover the contents as well as damage to the inside of your unit, including walls, windows, and doors. There are several types of insurance, including replacement-cost, all-risk comprehensive, and personal liability. It is also wise to get insurance to cover deficiencies in the condominium corporation's insurance coverage in the event of fire so that any damage to your unit could be repaired in full; otherwise the unit owners would have to pay on a proportional basis any deficiency by means of a special assessment. You should also carry sufficient liability insurance.

Many insurance companies have developed a specialized program referred to as condominium homeowner's package insurance. Check in the Yellow Pages under "Insurance Brokers" and compare coverage and costs. Refer to chapter 5 for a more detailed discussion of insurance protection.

Unit Repair and Maintenance Costs

You will have to allocate a certain amount of your personal financial budget to repair and maintenance needs relating to the inside of your unit. Your monthly assessment fee would cover common elements outside your unit only. Your portion of this cost is usually determined by means of a unit entitlement.

Unit entitlement is the basis on which the owner's contribution to the common expenses or maintenance fees of the condominium corporation are calculated. Various formulas are used for the calculation. In some developments,

the percentage calculated for the unit's share is determined by the original purchase price of each unit in relation to the value of the total property. Another
method is to apportion costs on the basis of the number of units in equal proportion, regardless of unit size. But the most common formula is to calculate the
unit entitlement by dividing the number of square feet in an owner's unit by the
number of square feet in all the units.

For example, let's say a condominium development contains 15 condominium units, the total square feet of all units is 15,680, your individual unit
is 784 square feet, and the annual cost to maintain the common elements and
other related expenses is $60,000. Then to calculate your monthly financial
commitment you would go through the following steps:

- Calculate your unit entitlement (784 ÷ 15,680 = 1/20 share in the
  common property)

- Calculate the annual share of maintenance costs (1/20 x $60,000 =
  $3,000 per year)

- Calculate the monthly share of maintenance costs (1/12 x $3,000 =
  $250 per month)

Utilities

You are responsible for your own utilities that you use in your unit, including
hydro, water, heat, etc. In apartment condominiums, these expenses are usually
included in the maintenance fee, whereas townhouse condominiums tend to
be separately metered and you are billed directly and individually by the utility
companies.

3

Financing Strategies for Your Condo

This chapter will help you find the right mortgage for your needs, in the amount you want, at the best interest rate and terms, and will show you how to save money in the process. You will also learn about other features and options you need to know when looking at financing your condo, and the factors that impact on interest rates.

Tip #15: Understand How Federal Government Policy Impacts Interest Rates

The federal government, through the Bank of Canada (Central Bank), sets the prime bank rate. This is the rate that the central bank charges on loans to financial institutions. The rate is set each week, generally at 25 basis points above the average yield (interest return) on three-month treasury bills. The government auctions these bills weekly. One hundred basis points represents 1% interest; therefore, 25 basis points would represent 0.25% interest. Conventional lenders (banks, trust companies, and credit unions) adjust their prime rates and mortgage rates using the federal bank rate as a guide. The Central Bank rate, therefore, sets a trend throughout the system.

There are various factors and political/economic dynamics that influence the federal bank rate. Here are two key ones:

- If the government is attempting to stimulate the economy because of a slowdown, it may lower rates throughout the money system by lowering the Central Bank rate. Conversely, if the economy is too buoyant and there is too much debt piling up, the Central Bank could slow spending by increasing the Central Bank rate, which would translate into higher lending rates at the banks.

- Government treasury bills or bonds are sold to international investors, among others. These investors place their money where they believe they will be getting their best return on their money. The highest interest rate, relative to other federal government rates for bills or bonds, or for that matter provincial bond issues, will naturally be attractive. This is relative, of course, to the perception of the investor of the stability of the currency and the economic and political stability of the government and the country as a whole. If there is uncertainty or concern in these areas—for example, the size of the national debt and current or projected budget deficit—investors might get nervous. If the government wants to attract more investors, for example, it has to increase its interest rate for bonds. If there is weak demand for treasury bills because of financial market volatility, this will affect the value of the Canadian dollar relative to the U.S. dollar and other currencies. For example, if the Canadian dollar depreciates 10 cents relative to the U.S. dollar, then investors might expect a jump in interest rates to offset the net reduction in yield received by the investor.

These factors can influence the short- and long-term interest rates of mortgages at any given time. This is why when you are getting a mortgage, for example, you may wish to have a six-month open mortgage if you think interest rates are decreasing, and then convert it into a three- or five-year closed mortgage when you see that interest rates are heading up. This is just one of many considerations you have to take into account when determining your mortgage needs and selection. Other factors to consider are covered below.

Tip #16: Why the Money Supply Affects Mortgage Rates

There is a natural connection between real estate sales growth/slowdown to the general economic cycle. (Real estate cycles are discussed in chapter 4.) When lenders have an excess supply of money to lend due to an inflow of customer deposits, for example, at RRSP purchase deadline time, then interest rates tend to be more attractive and competitive. This is because the lender needs to make money—that is, a "spread" on the difference between what it pays the depositor and what it charges for lending money. This spread could be 1% to 2% or more depending on various factors, including competition. Depositors must earn enough money on their savings to be comparable to the returns that they would earn on other investments, relative to the same degree of risk and liquidity.

Lenders realize that consumers do shop to get the best rate. They read information published daily on mortgage rates of various banks, mortgage companies, and credit unions. In addition, the Internet has many websites that post interest rates and offer online mortgage applications for quotes.

When people place money in a savings account, a pool of mortgage money is created. A situation where the inflow of deposit funds is high and the interest rates are low, and the lender has funds to lend, is referred to as a "loose money" market. This affects the real estate market, of course. In this situation, real estate activity can be expected to increase because more people will be able to afford financing and purchase a home or other real estate investment. More activity in the marketplace means a dynamic of supply and demand, and real estate prices can be expected to rise.

On the other hand, if the public thinks it can get a better return on other forms of investment than deposit funds, in a low-interest rate situation, for example, then as a consequence lenders are left with a shortage of money to lend for mortgage or other loans. This is referred to as a "tight money" market. The lender may reduce lending mortgage funds in many cases and be selective where the money is lent. Developers and contractors could have difficulty getting funds to build and, therefore, real estate activity slows down. As potential purchasers could have difficulty getting funds or may choose to hold off, real estate prices could drop due to the reduced demand. If mortgage interest rates are too high, many people may not be able to afford to buy as they may not qualify for a sufficient mortgage.

Tip #17: Know that Rates Vary Among Lenders

Rates vary among lenders, depending on their policies and restrictions. A more conservative lender may charge a higher rate than another. In general terms, conventional lenders (e.g., banks, trust companies, and credit unions) tend to be fairly competitive in the rates they charge for mortgages. A private mortgage lender generally wants a greater profit and therefore will charge more.

Tip #18: What Kind of Borrower Are You?

Lenders assess the creditworthiness of the borrower and the ability to pay. A borrower who has few assets, has only recently become employed or is self-employed, or has a spotty credit record, will pay a higher rate of interest than a borrower who has the opposite profile. For example, this is graphically reflected in the case of loans to a business. The lowest risk/no risk customer could receive the prime rate of interest (lowest) for a loan. Higher-risk businesses could be paying prime +1% to prime +8%, if they can get any funds at all.

Tip #19: Different Properties Mean Different Rates

After the lender has appraised the property, assessed the type of location and the resale potential of the property, and determined the amount of equity the borrower has, the lender will set the mortgage rate. Properties that are recreational, rural, speculative, or raw land will either be turned down or be approved at a higher interest rate. Frequently, in this latter situation, the lender will require higher owner equity and lower lender debt. Conversely, if the place you are buying is a house or condo in an economically stable community, you would probably obtain a competitive rate.

Tip #20: Know the Mortgage Hierarchy

This issue is discussed in more detail later in this section. Basically, the security of the mortgage is greater depending on its date of registration relative to other mortgages. A mortgage that is registered first is referred to as a first mortgage, a mortgage that is registered second in line is referred to as a second mortgage, and so on. In the event that the borrower defaults on a mortgage and the property is sold, the first mortgage gets paid out first from the proceeds, followed by the second, etc. Therefore, the lower the mortgage ranks in terms of priority the higher the risk to the lender that it will lose money if there is a shortfall on sale.

There is a direct relationship between risk and interest rate. A first mortgage could be at 6%, a second at 10%, and a third at 14%. How much equity the owner has is also a factor. If the owner has lots of equity, no matter how many mortgages on the property, the lower the risk to the last lender of losing money on a forced sale.

Tip #21: How the Mortgage Term Is Connected to the Interest Rate

There is a more detailed discussion of mortgage terms shortly. The interest rate is affected by such factors as:

- The amortization period (that is, the length of time over which the mortgage is paid out in full).

- Whether the mortgage is insured by CMHC or Genworth Financial Canada (if there is a lower risk, there is a lower rate).

- The length of the term before the mortgage is due for payment or renegotiation (e.g., six months, five years, or longer). Generally speaking, the longer the term, the more the risk of uncertainty about interest rates for the lender over that extended period; therefore, the rate is higher, as a protective buffer. This is not always the case, however.

- Whether the mortgage is open. If it is open, it can be paid at any time before the end of the term without penalty. If closed, it cannot be repaid or can be repaid but with a penalty (usually three months' interest or interest differential for the balance of the term, whichever is greater). Open mortgages have higher interest rates; closed mortgages have lower interest rates.

- Whether the interest rate is calculated and compounded annually, semi-annually or monthly. The more frequent the interest calculation and compounding, the higher the effective rate of interest that you will be paying.

- The frequency of your payment schedule (e.g., weekly, bimonthly, monthly, etc.).

Tip #22: How to Determine the Maximum Mortgage You Can Afford

Different lenders have different criteria for approving the amount of mortgage funds available. There is considerable flexibility with many lenders and it is important to compare or have a mortgage broker do so on your behalf in order to get the maximum amount of mortgage funds possible in your situation.

Lenders use the Gross Debt Service Ratio and Total Debt Service Ratio as standard formulas for determining mortgage qualification. There are other forms of calculation that you may want to use that would be helpful to you in determining the data relating to mortgages.

In calculating matters of principal and interest relating to mortgages and other factors such as different pay periods, you may want to obtain an amortization table or mortgage interest booklet, from a bank or another lending institution, or simply use the Internet.

Gross Debt Service Ratio (GDS Ratio)

The GDS Ratio is used to calculate the amount you can afford to spend for mortgage principal (P) and interest (I) payments. Some lenders also include property taxes (T) as part of this formula, and possibly heating costs (H) as well. All these expenses are added together. Under the GDS Ratio, payments generally should not exceed 30% of your income. There is flexibility in lending criteria, though, as some lenders will go up to 32% and in some cases 35% of your income and only include P and I rather than PIT or PITH.

Total Debt Service Ratio (TDS Ratio)

Many people have monthly financial obligations other than paying a mortgage and taxes, and lenders want to know what these are in order to determine someone's ability to debt-service a mortgage. Using the TDS Ratio, the bank would want to know your fixed monthly debts such as credit card payments, car payments, other loans, and condominium maintenance fees. In general terms, no more than 40% of your gross family income can be used when calculating the amount you can afford to pay for principal, interest, and taxes, plus your fixed monthly debts. The lender is naturally concerned about minimizing the risk that you potentially might be unable to meet your financial obligations relating to the mortgage, if the ratio of income to debt is too high.

It is important for you to roll in all your monthly expenses, some of which may not be taken into account by the lender, so that you get an accurate picture of your financial standing. These costs can include groceries, utilities, child support, and insurance, for example. Make sure you do a personal cost-of-living budget. This should give you a fairly specific idea, net of tax, of what your monthly income is and what your monthly debt-servicing charges will be on top of financing a mortgage.

Tip #23: You Own the Property When the Mortgage Is Dead

A *mortgage* is a contract between one party who wants to borrow money and another party who wants to lend money. The borrower is referred to as the *mortgagor,* and the lender is referred to as the *mortgagee.* These terms can sometimes be confusing. The terms *borrower* and *lender* are also used. The mortgage agreement states that in exchange for the money which the lender is providing, the borrower will provide security to the lender in the form of a mortgage document to be filed against the property.

For the purposes of this book, the term *property* will refer to the actual unit (whether a townhouse, condominium, an apartment, or a detached unit) and the portion of ownership in the common property. The mortgage document specifies the rights that the lender has to the property in the event of default on the terms of the mortgage by the borrower. The types of remedies that the mortgagee has against the mortgagor will be covered later in this part.

A mortgage document filed against the title of the property in the appropriate provincial land registry provides security to the mortgagee against other creditors which the mortgagor may have. If a *first mortgage is* filed against the property and the mortgagee checks to make sure that there are no other encumbrances or charges against the property, then the amount outstanding on the first mortgage takes priority over any and all other creditors (i.e., it is paid off first from the sale of the property on default).

Additional loans could be obtained by the mortgagor in which additional mortgages are filed against the property; a *second* or *third* or *fourth* mortgage could be filed against the property. Each mortgage ranks lower in priority than the previous, as the date of registration is the criterion that determines priority. Because of the increasing risk involved for subsequent mortgages, higher interest rates are charged. For example, the first mortgage interest rate may be 6%; the second, 9%; the third, 13%; and the fourth, 20%. The first mortgage would be paid out in full from any proceeds of sale, followed by the second mortgage and so on. It is possible that the price a home would sell for may only cover the payout on the first and second mortgages in this example, leaving no funds available to pay out the third and fourth.

Mortgages are regulated by federal and provincial law. Although the laws may be different from one province to another, the description of a mortgage outlined in this book applies to most mortgages. The method of mortgage registration and the enforcement laws are the main areas of variation between provinces. Some of the common clauses in a mortgage are discussed next.

The difference between the amount that the condominium could be sold for and what you still owe on your mortgages is referred to as your *equity*. The quicker you pay down your principal, the more equity you will have. Take advantage of options that allow you to reduce principal outside of regular payments.

Tip #24: Know the Fine Print Before You Sign

Most mortgage documents are in fine print and are fairly detailed. Do not assume that all mortgage documents are the same. The only way you can fully understand your mortgage contract is to have a competent and experienced real estate lawyer review it and interpret the key areas for you. In addition to differences in mortgage contracts, laws are always changing.

Many people sign mortgages without having any idea what is in them. This is a recipe for disaster. The purpose of this section is to outline some of the terms that you should be familiar with so that you will be better prepared when discussing your mortgage—before you sign it—with a lawyer.

In any mortgage, there are these basic provisions: the date of the mortgage, the names of the parties who are signing, a legal description of the property, the amount of the loan, the payment terms including interest and frequency, the respective obligations of the lender and the borrower, and the signatures of all the parties. Some of the common clauses that you may find in the mortgage are discussed below. Note that **special clauses relating to a condominium purchase** will be covered below under the tips in this section on types of mortgages.

a) Personal Guarantee

Under a mortgage, the borrower is personally liable for the debt to the lender. In the event of default, the lender can sue the borrower for the full amount of the mortgage; the lender is not obliged to commence foreclosure proceedings and take over the property or sell the property. In practical terms, however, the lender normally commences a form of foreclosure action to protect its interest as well as suing the borrower personally. If the property is sold, then the borrower would be responsible for the shortfall plus all the associated legal and other costs which the lender has incurred.

If you have a *co-covenantor* on the mortgage—someone else who covenants or promises that he will meet all the obligations of the mortgage—the lender can sue both the borrower and the co-covenantor for the debt under the mortgage. Sometimes the term *guarantor is* used instead of *co-covenantor.* In practical terms they are inter-changeable. The lender may refuse to give funds covered by a mortgage without extra security protection by means of an additional guarantor or co-covenantor.

If you are married and are purchasing the condominium under your personal name, the lender will almost always insist on your spouse's signing as a guarantor or co-covenantor, regardless of your creditworthiness. This is to protect the lender under the matrimonial or family relations legislation of the province: in the event that a separation or divorce occurs, the lender does not want its property security to be compromised.

b) Insurance

This clause requires that the mortgagor insure the condominium against fire. The insurance policy must show that the mortgagee is entitled to be paid first from the mortgage proceeds in the event of a claim on the policy.

There is also a provision in the mortgage which sets out the amount of the insurance (replacement). It states that if you fail to pay the premium, the mortgagee can do so, or if you fail to get sufficient insurance, the mortgagee can do so, and all the additional premium costs can be added onto the principal amount of debt of your mortgage.

c) Maintain Property

This clause in the mortgage states that you are required to keep the property in good repair. The reason for this provision is that the lender obviously does not want the property to deteriorate through neglect and therefore reduce its property value, compromising the value of the security.

d) Requirement to Pay Taxes

This clause states that you are obliged to pay all property taxes when they become due, and that if you do not do so, the lender is entitled to pay the taxes and add the amount paid in taxes to the principal of the mortgage. Many lenders attempt to avoid any problem with taxes by having a separate tax account set up at the time you take out the mortgage. This means that you pay an extra amount every month on your payment to the bank for a tax portion which goes into that account, and once a year the lender pays the property taxes directly. In many cases you can negotiate out of this prepayment provision and look after the taxes yourself. Some lenders require proof that taxes are current and have been paid every year.

e) Requirement to Keep Any Subsequent Mortgages in Good Standing

This provision states that you must maintain all of your financial obligations on the second and third mortgages so that they do not go into default. If they do go into default, foreclosure proceedings could occur. If the property was sold, the first mortgage would be paid off first, followed by the second and the third. This will be discussed in more detail later in this chapter, in Tips #37 and #38.

f) Prohibition Against Renting Out Premises

Some mortgage documents state very clearly that the whole premises cannot be rented out. This is fairly common with CMHC residential mortgages, as they are generally granted for the benefit of the owner/occupier and not for investment or rental purposes. However, there are exceptions, and the policy does not prevent renting a suite in the house as a mortgage helper.

g) Must Comply with All Laws

This provision would advise that all federal, provincial, and municipal laws concerning the use and occupancy of the property must be fully complied with. This is an important provision if you are intending to rent out the property. There may be a prohibition against renting the property if it is not zoned for that purpose. This is common in recreational areas. Some municipal zoning bylaws prohibit rental of secondary suites in the primary single family residence. You need to check out your rights before you buy, by obtaining advice from an experience real estate lawyer.

h) No Urea Formaldehyde Foam Insulation (UFFI)

Many mortgages state that no UFFI is permitted in the premises at the time the mortgage is granted or subsequently.

i) Prepayment Privileges

It is important that you make sure the prepayment privileges are set out clearly in the agreement.

j) Assumption of Mortgage Privileges

Assumption of mortgage privileges should be set out clearly in the mortgage document. This subject also has been discussed earlier.

k) Quiet Possession

This provision states that unless the mortgagor defaults, the mortgagee will not interfere in any way with the peaceful enjoyment of the property by the mortgagor. In practical terms this means that the mortgagee cannot enter the premises.

l) Acceleration Clause

This clause states that if the mortgagor defaults on any of the terms of the mortgage agreement, then at the option of the mortgagee the full amount outstanding on the principal of the mortgage plus interest is immediately due and payable. This clause is not applicable in all provinces.

m) Default

The steps that can occur on mortgage default will be covered later in this section.

Always, always have your lawyer advise you on the contents of the mortgage before signing it.

Tip #25: How a Pre-approved Mortgage Can Help You

You have probably heard about pre-approved mortgages. This concept is fairly popular with most conventional lending institutions and credit unions, and through mortgage brokers and online mortgage companies. The purpose is to give you a precise amount of money that you can rely on for mortgage purposes when you are out searching to buy a home and negotiating a purchase. You are given a fixed amount of mortgage for a period of time, for example, $100,000 with an interest rate that would be guaranteed for generally 60, 75, or 90 days, depending on the market conditions. There is always a condition, of course, that the lender must approve the actual property being purchased, before you can enact a final contractual offer to purchase. This provides the lender with an opportunity to make sure that the security is suitable.

Tip #26: Where to Find Conventional Financing

There are several varieties of mortgages available from banks, credit unions, trust companies, mortgage companies, private lenders, government, and the vendor. Although most homeowners obtain financing through a conventional mortgage, it is helpful to be aware of other alternatives.

Conventional Mortgage

The conventional mortgage is the most common type of financing for residential property. It is fairly standard in its terms and conditions, although there can be variations. In this type of mortgage, the loan cannot exceed 75% of the appraised value or purchase price of the property, whichever is the lesser of the two. This requirement is governed by law. The purchaser is responsible for raising the other 25% of the funds necessary, either through a down payment or through other means such as a second mortgage or vendor-back mortgage. Conventional mortgages are available through most financial institutions, including banks, trust companies, and credit unions. In most cases these mortgages do not have to be insured, but occasionally a lender may require it. For example, if the property is older or is smaller than is normally required by the policy of the lender, or if it is located in a rural or a run-down area, then the mortgage may be required to be insured with the Canada Mortgage and Housing Corportion (CMHC) or Genworth Financial Canada. CMHC is a federal Crown corporation, whereas Genworth is a private corporation.

High-ratio/Insured Mortgage

If you are unable to raise the necessary 25% funding to complete the purchase of the home, then a high-ratio mortgage may be available to you. This is a conventional mortgage which exceeds the 75% limit referred to earlier. By law, these mortgages must be insured, and they are available only through approved lenders that are accepted by CMHC or Genworth Financial. CMHC has specific guidelines for qualifying, but the administration is done through the bank or credit union.

High-ratio mortgages are available for up to 90% of the purchase price or of the appraisal, whichever is the lower, and in some cases 95%. In fact, in some cases, if you are a first-time homebuyer, you might be able to obtain 100% financing. The percentage for which you would be eligible depends on various circumstances. There are also restrictions on the purchase price of the home that may be involved. Obtain further information from your realtor, banker, or mortgage holder, or CMHC or Genworth Financial Canada directly. (Contact information for CMHC and Genworth Financial is provided in the Appendix.)

Collateral Mortgage

In a collateral mortgage the mortgage security is secondary, or collateral, to some other main form of security taken by the lender. This main security may take the form of a promissory note, personal guarantee, or assignment of some other form of security that the lender may require. A collateral mortgage is therefore a backup protection of the loan which is filed against the property. The payment requirements on the loan are covered in the promissory note, and once the promissory note has been paid off in full, the collateral mortgage will automatically be paid off. You would then be entitled to have the collateral mortgage discharged from the title of the property.

One of the main differences between a collateral mortgage and a conventional mortgage is that a conventional mortgage can be assumed, whereas a collateral mortgage, of course, cannot be, as it is subject to some other form of security between the parties. Otherwise, the terms of the collateral mortgage could be very similar to the debt of a conventional mortgage. The money borrowed on a collateral mortgage could be used for the purchase of the property itself, or for other purposes such as home improvements, a business investment, or a vacation.

Government-assisted Mortgages

National Housing Act (NHA) mortgages are loans granted under the provisions of this federal act. They are administered through CMHC. You can apply for an NHA loan at any chartered bank or credit union. Borrowers must pay an application fee to CMHC, which usually includes the cost of a property appraisal and an insurance fee. The latter is usually added to the principal amount of the mortgage, though it may be paid at the time of closing. Contact CMHC or your financial institution for the most current information on borrowing requirements.

In addition, some provinces have second mortgage funding available for home purchases. Generally there is a limit on the amount of the purchase price of the home, and a ceiling on the amount of the mortgage. Obtain further information from your realtor or lending institution.

Secondary Financing

Secondary financing generally consists of a second mortgage and possibly a third mortgage. One of the reasons why you may wish to take out a second mortgage is because the existing first mortgage you are assuming has an attractive interest rate or has other desirable features, and because there will be a shortfall between the amount of your available down payment and the amount of the first mortgage. You therefore need to obtain funds. Chartered banks will usually provide money for second mortgages up to a limit of 75% of the lower of the purchase price and the appraised value.

You can also obtain second mortgages through mortgage brokers or other sources that could go up as high as 90%, or more, of the purchase price or appraised value, whichever is lower. If the second mortgage has a term that is longer than that of the first mortgage you assume, make sure that you have a *postponement clause* put into the second mortgage. With this clause you would be able to automatically renew or replace the first mortgage when it becomes due without having to obtain the permission from the second mortgage lender to do so. In other words, if you reviewed the mortgage or obtained a replacement first mortgage, that mortgage would still be in first position, ahead of the second mortgage.

Assumed Mortgage

In the case of an assumed mortgage, you are qualified by the lender to assume an existing mortgage on the property. In some instances mortgages can be assumed with qualifications. If you assume the existing mortgage, it will save you the cost of legal fees and disbursements for registering the mortgage, obtaining appraisal, and other expenses. Whenever you are assuming an existing mortgage, it is important that your lawyer obtain for you a mortgage assumption statement showing the principal balance outstanding, the method of paying taxes, the remaining term on the mortgage and a copy of the mortgage which shows other features such as prepayment privileges, etc.

If you are a seller of the property, you should be very cautious about someone assuming your mortgage unless you obtain a release in writing from the lender that you will not be liable under the mortgage in the event that the person assuming it defaults on his obligations. In the event of default, the lender would be entitled to go after the original mortgagor as well as the person who assumed the mortgage, for the full amount of the debt outstanding or any shortfall after foreclosure proceedings and sale of the property has taken place. In an increasing real estate market, the risk could be low. However, in a declining real estate market, you don't need the grief, uncertainty, or risk. Since you can't predict the market, make sure you obtain the release from the bank. Otherwise, don't permit the assumption.

Make sure that you obtain legal advice before permitting any buyer to assume your mortgage.

Builder's Promotional Mortgage

In order to entice a sale for a new home or condominium, a builder sometimes tries to make financing easy for you by various means.

One way is by means of a discounted mortgage. In other words, to make the condo price attractive, the mortgage rate might be reduced to 4%, whereas the prevailing interest rate for a first mortgage could be 6%. The builder is able to "buy down" a mortgage from a lender at an attractive rate by paying a discount—the difference in financial terms between what the lender would make on a 6% mortgage and what they would make on a 4% mortgage.

However, builders frequently add on this discount to the purchase price of the home. You could be paying a lower interest rate because you are paying for a higher purchase price than you otherwise would have to pay. Another factor to be aware of is that the discounted mortgage may only be for a short time (e.g., a year), and after that period you will have to obtain your own mortgage at the prevailing rate. Thus, although a discounted mortgage could initially appear attractive, over the long term it could be false economy. For example, you might prefer a 5-, 7- or 10-year fixed rate mortgage. If you have a first mortgage that expires in a year and you need to renew the mortgage, the interest rate could have gone up by then.

Another type of financing a builder could offer is to have a promo mortgage package for any buyer arranged through the lender that the builder is using for the condo project financing. This would provide more business for the builder's lender, which could result in a better deal for the builder's financing costs or even a commission incentive. For example, the builder's lender could offer the buyer a 1/2% point less than the posted rate for a mortgage and include all legal costs for transferring title and doing the mortgage work. However, you need to be wary and do your due diligence and check with a mortgage broker. You could find that in a competitive mortgage marketplace, you could get a better deal, for example, 1% point less than the posted mortgage rate and including all your legal costs as an incentive.

You may also be exposed to a "phantom mortgage." See the Glossary.

Tip #27: Alternate Sources of Financing

Vendor Mortgage

A vendor mortgage is sometimes referred to as a vendor-back or vendor take-back mortgage. Here, the vendor encourages the sale of the property by giving the purchaser a loan on the purchase of the property. For example, if the purchaser is able to get 75% conventional financing but does not have sufficient funds for a down payment of 25%, the vendor may be prepared to give, in effect, a second mortgage for 15% of the purchase price. That way, the purchaser would only need to come up with a 10% down payment. The purchaser would then make mortgage payments to the vendor as if a normal commercial lender held the second mortgage.

If you are the purchaser, it is fairly common for the vendor not to make any credit check or any other financial assessment of you. On the other hand, if you are the vendor, for obvious reasons you should make sure that there is a provision in the offer to purchase that you can do a thorough credit check of the purchaser before deciding on granting the second mortgage. You will need to obtain permission from the borrower in writing. Equifax is one of the major credit reporting agencies in Canada. (Refer to the Appendix for Helpful Websites.)

Sometimes the vendor makes arrangements through a mortgage broker for the second mortgage to be sold at a discount as soon as the transaction is complete. This way, the vendor gets cash immediately, minus, of course, the cost required to discount the mortgage and the broker's fee. Generally the mortgage has to have a fixed and not a floating rate if it is to be sold, and the terms should be at least a year to be attractive to a purchaser of the mortgage. If the vendor intends to sell the vendor-back mortgage, there is normally a precondition in it that the purchaser will cooperate with any credit checks and will agree to the mortgage being assigned. Also, that acceptance of the offer to purchase is based on a commitment from a mortgage broker that there is a purchaser for the second mortgage as soon as the sale completes.

If you are considering providing a mortgage-back, again it is important to be cautious and obtain legal advice in advance. There is a risk that the purchaser will refuse to pay on the second mortgage if there appears to be any problem with the condition of the property after the sale. Naturally the vendor or the assignee of the vendor's second mortgage could commence foreclosure proceedings, but in practical terms it is possible that the purchaser could attempt to raise various legal defences. To discuss in any detail these types of problems is outside the scope of this book; they are raised merely to alert the reader to the need for competent legal advice in these unique situations.

Blanket Mortgage

A blanket mortgage, sometimes referred to as an "inter alia" mortgage, is a type of mortgage registered over two or more properties. The purpose behind the mortgage is to provide the lender with additional property as security. It is normally used where a borrower wants more money than the lender is prepared to provide on the basis of one property alone. That property may not have sufficient equity and, for example, the amount of money that is being requested could constitute 90% or 95% of the value of the first property. If the second property has attractive equity, the lender may be prepared to advance the funds to the borrower but have one mortgage filed against both properties. In the event of default, the lender could proceed against one or both of the properties in order to get sufficient proceeds from the sale to satisfy the outstanding debt.

Blanket mortgages are very common in condominium projects. The developer normally has a blanket mortgage over all the individual units and common areas. On the basis of this blanket mortgage, a lender will advance funds for the completion of the project. As soon as a unit is sold, the lender releases the portion of the blanket mortgage that was filed on the title of that unit in order for the purchaser of the unit to place his own mortgage. The developer normally has a requirement with its lender that all or a portion (e.g., 50% or 75%) of the purchase price of the condominium unit has to be paid to the lender to reduce the blanket mortgage as a condition for the lender's releasing the encumbrance on that unit.

Leasehold Mortgage

A leasehold mortgage is a mortgage on a house or condominium where the land is rented rather than owned. The mortgage must be amortized over a period that is shorter than the length of the land lease. Normally a lender will not grant a mortgage on leasehold property unless the duration of the lease is of sufficient length that the risk is fairly minimal to the lender. For example, if a condominium is on leasehold land with a 99-year lease and there are 85 years left on the lease, then there is relatively little risk to the lender. On the other hand, if the leasehold is for a 30-year period and there are five years left on the lease, the lender will consider the risk too high, because at the end of the five-year period the lease will expire and therefore there is no right or entitlement to the leasehold interest. This would mean that the condominium would have no value to a potential purchaser after five years.

Agreement for Sale

An agreement for sale is not actually a mortgage, but it is another way of financing a sale. It should not be confused with an agreement for purchase and sale. An agreement for sale is normally used in a situation wherein the buyer of the property does not have sufficient funds for a down payment and the vendor wishes to dispose of the property. In an agreement for sale, the vendor finances the purchase of the property in a fashion similar to that of a vendor-back mortgage. The purchaser, though, does not become the legal owner of the property until the agreement for sale has been paid in full. At that time the purchaser is legally entitled to have the conveyance of the legal interest of the property transferred over to the purchaser. In the meantime, the vendor remains the registered owner on title of the property. The purchaser has the legal right of possession, and makes regular payments to the vendor under the terms of the agreement between the vendor and the purchaser. The purchaser has a legal "right to purchase" which is registered against the title of the property in the provincial land registry office.

The terms of an agreement for sale are in many ways very similar to the terms found in a mortgage. The agreement for sale may have a five-year term, for example, in which time the full amount is due and payable. At that time either the purchaser has to arrange conventional mortgage financing or another form of financing to pay off the vendor, or else make an agreement with the vendor for an extension of the agreement for sale for another term. Agreements for sale are frequently used where the purchaser cannot qualify to assume the existing mortgage or to obtain a new mortgage; in effect, the purchaser assumes a mortgage that would otherwise be un-assumable.

Tip #28: Understanding the Special Clauses in a Condominium Mortgage

In many cases, condominium mortgages are identical to any of the other mortgages discussed in terms of the provisions, except for a few special provisions in view of the unique nature of a condominium. Although a purchaser of a condominium receives legal title to one individual unit, the purchaser also has an undivided interest in the common elements of the development.

Some of the special clauses contained in most condominium mortgages that distinguish this type of mortgage from a conventional house mortgage are as follows:

- The lender has the right to use the unit owner's vote or consent in the condominium corporation. In other words, the lender has a proxy to vote in place of the borrower. In practical terms, the lender does not usually vote on any and all decisions in normal circumstances. The lender, though, does require that the borrower provide notice of all condominium corporation meetings, including special or extraordinary meetings announced by the condominium corporation, and copies of minutes and information.

- The lender requires that the borrower comply with all the terms of the bylaws, rules, and regulations of the condominium corporation. Any default on the borrower's part will constitute default under the mortgage.

- The lender requires the borrower to pay all costs of maintenance of the common elements. In the event of failure of the borrower to do so, the tender is entitled to pay the costs on behalf of the borrower and add these onto the principal amount outstanding on the mortgage, with interest charged to this amount.

Tip #29: Where to Begin Shopping for a Mortgage

It is important to keep in mind that the competition for mortgage lending is extremely intense. There are numerous lenders of mortgage funds and they are all attempting to attract the customer to use their services. You should therefore do thorough research before deciding on which mortgage lender to use. Major city newspapers tend to publish a comparison of the prevailing mortgage rates by institution in the real estate section of the weekend newspaper. This will save you a lot of research time. Also check with mortgage brokers in your community. They frequently publish a list of current comparative rates and will send a copy to you free upon request. Also, check on the Internet for comparative and competitive rates. Most mortgage brokers, and online mortgage brokers or lenders, post all their current rates on their websites.

The main sources of mortgage funds available to residential purchases that you may wish to consider are listed below, some of which are discussed at length.

- *Commercial banks*
- *Trust companies*
- *Credit unions*
- *Government:* As mentioned earlier, the federal government, through CMHC, provides mortgage funds if you qualify. In addition, some provincial governments have second mortgage funding available, again if you qualify.
- *A vendor-back mortgage*
- *Assumption of an existing mortgage*
- *Obtaining of funds from personal sources such as family, relatives, friends, or business associates.*
- *Mortgage companies:* Check in the Yellow Pages or Internet under "Mortgages."
- *Real estate companies:* Some real estate companies may refer you to lenders or mortgage brokers.
- *Condominium development companies:* Many of these companies have made financing packages available to purchasers of new condominiums through banks or credit unions.

Tip #30: Using a Mortgage Broker

Mortgage lending has become very complex, with constantly changing rates, terms, and conditions. Each lending institution has its own criteria that it applies to potential borrowers. Some insist on a particular type of property as security, while others require a certain quality or type of applicant. In this latter case, factors such as type of employment, job stability, income, and credit background are weighed. There is a broad range of philosophies and policies held by the various lending institutions on the issue of security and applicant qualifications in order for a lender to advance mortgage funds.

Other factors also impact on mortgage approval. Availability or shortage of funds, past experience in a specific area, perceived resale market for a particular property, and the attitude of the lending committee (if a credit union) are all factors which could affect approving a mortgage.

Mortgage brokers make it their business to know all the various plans and lending policies and the lender's attitude on various aspects of mortgage security and covenants. A mortgage broker is in effect a matchmaker in the mortgage money market, attempting to introduce the appropriate lender to the purchaser. Mortgage brokers have access to numerous sources of funds, including conventional lenders such as banks and credit unions, as well as:

- CMHC
- private pension funds
- union pension funds
- real estate syndication funds
- foreign bank subsidiaries
- insurance companies
- private lenders.

The broker knows all the lenders' objectives; the broker is therefore capable of matching the applicant and his property with the appropriate plan and lender. Alternatively, the broker can provide a series of mortgage plans from which the borrower may select the one that best suits his needs. If you are buying a condominium as your principal residence, you generally don't pay any fees, other than the appraisal fee to the mortgage broker. The broker receives a referral commission from the lender. Check the Yellow Pages or Internet under "Mortgage Brokers," and the Helpful Websites section in the Appendix for mortgage broker associations.

Tip #31: The Key Factors to Consider When Selecting a Mortgage

There are many factors you have to decide on before finalizing your mortgage decision. The key factors are amortization, term of the mortgage, open or closed mortgage, interest rate, payment schedules, prepayment privilege, and assumability. A brief explanation of each of these concepts follows:

Amortization

Amortization is the length of time over which the regular (usually monthly) payments have been calculated on the assumption that the mortgage will be fully paid over that period. The usual amortization period is 25 years, although there is a wide range of options available in 5-, 10-, 15-, 20-, and 30-year periods as well. Naturally, the shorter the amortization period, the more money you save on interest.

Term of the Mortgage

The term of the mortgage is the length of time the mortgagee will lend you the money. Terms may vary from 6 months to 10 years. If the amortization period was 25 years, that would mean that you have several different mortgages, possibly 10 to 20 separate terms, before you have completely paid off the loan.

At the end of each term, the principal and unpaid interest of the mortgage become due and payable. Unless you are able to repay the entire mortgage at this time, you would normally either renew the mortgage with the same lender on the same terms, renegotiate the mortgage depending on the options available to you at that time, or refinance the mortgage through a different lending institution. If you renew with a different mortgage lender, there could be extra administrative charges involved. Because there is considerable competition among lenders, frequently there will be no administrative fee if you transfer a mortgage to another institution. In some cases another institution will absorb the legal fees and costs as well, as an inducement for you to bring the business away from a competitive lender.

Some people take out short-term mortgages, e.g., for six months, anticipating that interest rates will go down and that at the end of six months there will be a lower interest rate. The problem is that if rates have gone up instead of down at the end of the six months, your monthly mortgage payment will increase and you may not be able to afford, or want to pay, the increased rates. The other option you have is to negotiate a long-term mortgage, e.g., for five years, so that you can budget for the future over a five-year period with certainty about the interest rates. The lender is not obliged to renew the mortgage at the end of the term. If the lender decides to renew, an administration fee of $100 to $250 is often charged. However, this is frequently waived by negotiation or due to competitive realities.

Open or Closed Mortgage

An *open* mortgage allows you to increase the payment of the amount of the principal at any time. You could pay off the mortgage in full at any time before the term is over without any penalty or extra charges. Because of this flexibility, open mortgages normally cost at least a percentage point more than standard closed mortgages.

A *closed* mortgage locks you in for the period of the term of the mortgage. There is a penalty fee for any advance payment. A straight closed mortgage will normally have a provision that if it is prepaid due to the property being sold or the death of the borrower, either a three-month interest penalty or the interest rate differential for the balance of the term, whichever is greater, will be applied. Alternatively, the penalty could be waived entirely, if the new purchaser of the property takes out a new mortgage with the lending institution. Some closed mortgages have a prepayment feature.

Interest Rate Options

There are various ways to calculate the interest: the *fixed rate,* which means the interest rate remains fixed for the period of the term of the mortgage (for example, one year), and the *variable rate,* which means that the interest rate could vary every week or month, according to the premium interest rate set by the lender every week or month. In this latter case, although the actual monthly payments that you make would usually stay the same, the interest charge proportion of that monthly payment of principal and interest will vary with that month's rate.

How often interest is *compounded*—in other words, the interest charged on interest owing—will determine the total amount of interest that you actually pay on your mortgage. Obviously, the more frequent the compounding of interest, the more interest you will pay. The lender can charge any rate of interest, within the law, and compound that at any frequency desired. That is why it is important for you to check on the nature of the compounding on interest.

By law, mortgages have to contain a statement showing the basis on which the rate of interest is calculated. Mortgage interest has traditionally been compounded on a half-yearly basis. If a mortgage is calculated on the basis of straight interest, that means there is no compounding, but just the running total of the interest outstanding at any point in time. Some mortgages, such as variable-rate mortgages, are compounded weekly or monthly. The rate quoted for a variable-rate mortgage is called a *nominal rate*, whereas the equivalent rate for "normal" mortgages (compounded semi-annually or annually) is called the *effective rate*. As an example, a mortgage which quotes a nominal rate of 5% has an effective rate of interest of 5% when compounded yearly, approximately 5.20% when compounded half-yearly, and approximately 5.40% when compounded monthly.

Interest Averaging

If you are considering assuming an existing first mortgage because the rate and term are attractive, but concerned about the current interest rate of second mortgage financing, do an interest average calculation. You might find the average interest rate to be quite acceptable. Here is an example of how you calculate it:

1st Mortgage $60,000 x 5% = $3,000
2nd Mortgage $30,000 x 8% = $2,400
$90,000 x y% = $5,400
Average interest rate y% = $5,400/$90,000 = 6%

Payment Schedules

There are many payment schedule options available in the marketplace, including weekly, biweekly (every two weeks), monthly, semi-annually, annually, and other variations. Generally, the more frequently you make payments, the lower the amount of interest that you will be paying. Obtain a computer printout from your lender or the Internet, showing the actual savings *before* you commit to making more frequent payments.

Depending on your negotiations with the lender, you may make payments on interest only, or have a graduated payment schedule, which means that at the beginning of the term of the mortgage your payments are lower and increase over time so that at the end of the term the payments will be considerably higher. The reason for this type of arrangement is that the ability of the borrower to pay the payment will be able to increase over time, and the payment schedules are graduated to accommodate that.

Normally payments made on the mortgage are a blend of principal and interest. These have traditionally been amortized assuming a monthly payment basis.

Prepayment Privilege

This is a very important feature to have if your mortgage is a fixed mortgage. If it is an open mortgage, you can pay the balance outstanding on the mortgage, in part or in full, at any time without penalty. If on the other hand you have a closed mortgage which does not have any prepayment privileges, you are locked in for the term of the mortgage, e.g., three years, without the privilege of prepaying without penalty.

You may therefore wish to have a mortgage which, though called a closed mortgage, is in fact partly open and partly closed, permitting prepayment at certain stages and in a certain manner, but not at other times. For example, you may be permitted to make a prepayment of between 10% and 20% annually on the principal amount outstanding. This could be made once a year at the end of each year of the mortgage, or at some point during the year, depending on the terms with the lender. Another variation would also give you the option of increasing the amount of your monthly payment by 10% to 20% once a year. You can see the incredible difference this would make in terms of saving on interest and reducing the amortization period. Every time a prepayment is made, or every time you increase your monthly payments, the balance owing, and thus the monthly cost of interest, is reduced. The net effect is that a larger portion of each payment will be applied toward the principal, since monthly (or other agreed-upon regular) payments usually remain the same.

Make sure that you completely understand your prepayment options, as they could save you a lot of money. It is important to make a realistic assessment of the right package of your needs. For example, ask whether the prepayment percentage you can apply is based on the original mortgage taken out, or the outstanding balance. It makes a big difference.

Assumability

Assumability means that the buyer takes over the obligation and payments under the vendor's mortgage. Most mortgage contracts deal with the issue of assumability very clearly. The lender can agree to full assumability without qualifications, assumability with qualifications, or no assumability. Generally, it is with qualifications.

The issue of assumability is an important one to consider. You would be able to have a wider range of potential purchasers interested in buying your home if a purchaser could assume the balance of the term (e.g., three years) of a low interest mortgage in a prevailing high interest mortgage environment.

Portability

Some lenders have a feature called portability. This means that if you sell one home and buy another during the term of your mortgage, you can transfer the mortgage from one property to the other. Check carefully, though. Some lenders require that you purchase the new house within a short period of time after you sell your original house, in order to qualify for this transfer or mortgage rate continuance option, e.g., two to four months. Other lenders require that you transfer the mortgage to your new home concurrently as you sell your old home. In practical terms, you could save money if interest rates have gone up before buying the new home. Otherwise, you would be taking out a new mortgage for your new home at current, higher mortgage rates, thereby resulting in lower mortgage amount availability.

Remember, the higher the interest rate, the lower the mortgage amount that you qualify for. Conversely, if mortgage rates have done down since you bought the first house, you would probably not be interested in transferring your existing mortgage unless you had a fixed-rate mortgage, with a mortgage differential penalty that was larger than the savings you would realize by taking out a new mortgage.

Tip #32: What You Need to Know When Applying for a Mortgage

In applying for a mortgage, there are various steps you should follow to make sure you obtain the funds you need on the terms and conditions you want. Many people go through a mortgage broker or apply online for a mortgage, which saves a lot of time and inconvenience, and generally gets the best rate due to the competitive marketplace.

Preparing for the Application Interview

Here is a summary of the steps that you should follow prior to any interview:

- Complete your comparison shopping of all the types of lending institutions that you could obtain mortgages from. Check competing interest rates for different types of mortgages by contacting a mortgage broker to obtain a current schedule. Refer to your local newspaper to see if it regularly prints comparative mortgage rates, check the Internet and mortgage brokers.

- Understand the jargon. This book should help you to know what you want from a mortgage, and therefore negotiate the package that is suited to your purposes.

- Determine the questions that you want to ask the lender.

- Determine your financial needs.

- Calculate the maximum amount of mortgage available that you might be able to expect from a lender.

- Obtain a letter of confirmation of employment from your employer, if you are employed. This would confirm your salary, your position, and the length of time you have been with that employer. If you are self-employed, you will be required to bring copies of recent financial statements or income tax returns.

- Prepare a statement of your assets and liabilities and net worth.

- Complete details on the amount of the down payment that you will be providing and where the funds are coming from. This last could include savings accounts, term deposits, Canada Savings Bonds, RRSPs, a family loan, an inheritance, a divorce settlement, proceeds from the sale of a house, or other sources.

- Complete the sample mortgage application form.

- Obtain a copy of the Agreement of Purchase and Sale.

The Application Process

The steps to this process are as follows:

- You have to personally attend at the lending institution, generally along with your spouse and any co-applicant or guarantor. Alternatively, you could do almost the entire mortgage procedure online, and then just meet at the mortgage lender's office.

- A formal mortgage application has to be completed. The application is typically divided into three main sections: description of the property, financial details relating to the purchase of the property, and personal financial information.

- Processing of the application by the lender normally takes between two and five business days.

During that time the lender will:

- Check your credit references and your credit rating.

- Verify the financial information you have given.

- Have the property appraised (at your cost).

- Assess your application within the lender's approval guidelines.

- Issue a formal commitment of approval in writing.

Tip #33: Understanding What the Lender Requires of You

Different lenders have different guidelines when assessing mortgage applications, but generally there are three main criteria: character, capacity, and collateral.

Character

The lender will be attempting to make an assessment of your credit history, and other factors as well, with a view to predicting how you will meet your obligations in the future. For example, do you regularly pay your bills on time? What is your credit rating in terms of your credit history in previous loans that you have had? Do you seem to be dependable in terms of the duration that you have been at your job, or have you had a different job every three or four months?

Capacity

The lender is concerned about your ability to meet your financial obligation, and will be concerned about such questions as: Does your GDS Ratio fall within their guidelines? What are your other debts and obligations? Is your income sufficient to handle the mortgage payments? Is your income stable, and does it appear as though it will continue to be so? If you are self-employed, do you have a three-year history of attractive net revenue?

Collateral

Lenders are very much concerned with knowing that the security which has been provided for a loan is sufficient to cover the loan in the event that it is not repaid. That is why they use their own appraisers for assessing the value of a property; generally they want to have a conservative appraisal of the property as an extra caution. The lender wants to be satisfied that the property being offered as security could be readily sold if necessary. When making an appraisal and therefore determining the value of the security that is being pledged as collateral, the following factors are considered: location, price, zoning, condition of the housing unit, quality of neighbourhood, size, appearance, municipal services available, and comparative condominium sales in the area.

Tip #34: Beware the Many Costs of Obtaining a Mortgage

There are numerous direct and indirect expenses related to obtaining a mortgage. Not all of the following expenses will apply in your case, but it is helpful to be aware of them. There are also additional expenses which are not covered in this section, since they really relate not to obtaining a mortgage but to purchasing a property and having the title of the property transferred over to your name. These types of costs are covered in chapter 4, and include legal fees and disbursements, provincial land transfer filing fees, and property purchase tax. Other potential expenses involved when purchasing a condominium include a new home warranty fee, condominium maintenance fee adjustment, utility connection charges, cost of repairs that may be required prior to occupancy, and moving expenses. (Refer to the Condo Purchase Expenses Checklist in the Appendix.)

Costs will vary considerably from one lender to another. The type of financing that you are obtaining will be a factor. The following sections discuss some of the most common expenses that you should consider and, if necessary, budget for.

Mortgage Application Fee

Some lenders charge a processing fee or set-up fee for their administrative expenses in the processing of your mortgage application. Avoid paying this type of fee if at all possible. Due to the highly competitive nature of the mortgage industry, many lenders do not charge any application fee for residential mortgage purposes. *Note:* If you are borrowing money for non-residential purposes, such as investing in property, this type of fee may or may not be applied, due to the potential extra amount of work that is required in assessing the loan application.

Appraisal Fee

The lender will obtain its own appraiser to determine the value of the security for mortgage purposes. The necessary fee is either paid by the borrower to the lender in advance at the time of application, or is taken from the mortgage proceeds by the lender. In any event, the borrower pays the cost of the appraisal. Generally lenders will not give you a copy of the appraisal, unless you specifically ask for it, or make it a condition of your mortgage with them.

There is a possibility that you could save on the appraisal fee under certain circumstances. For example, if a vendor or purchaser has already arranged for a professional appraiser to evaluate the property, and the appraisal is not over 60 to 90 days old, the lender may be prepared to accept the appraisal if it approves of the appraiser, and if property values have remained the same or increased since the appraisal was made. Also, in a competitive marketplace, you can negotiate directly with the lender, or through the mortgage broker, to have the fee waived and absorbed by the lender. Nothing ventured, nothing gained.

Survey Fee

If you are purchasing a condominium, you will not generally be required to obtain a property survey prior to mortgage funds being paid out. Surveys are generally required for single family homes. However, a lender usually requires a copy of the condominium plan, showing the location and dimensions of the condominium being purchased. For example, a condominium may show as 1,200 square feet in size, but a survey could show that 900 square feet of that is livable space and the other 300 square feet is a balcony; e.g., the balcony is not considered part of your unit ownership but is limited common elements.

Mortgage Insurance Premiums (CMHC or Genworth Financial Canada)

If you are obtaining a high-ratio mortgage or the lender requires you to obtain mortgage insurance for other reasons, then you will be paying a mortgage insurance fee. The fee normally ranges between 1/2% and 3% of the amount of the mortgage that is being insured and is either added onto the mortgage total or paid by you in a lump sum at the time of closing the mortgage transaction. Mortgage insurance was discussed earlier under the topic of high-ratio mortgages.

Condominium Fire Insurance Premiums

Lenders require that any borrower on a mortgage carry sufficient fire insurance to cover the amount of the mortgage, and that they be paid off first. The second mortgage lenders would want the same type of coverage and have it shown that they are paid off second, and so on. It is necessary for the borrower to purchase sufficient replacement insurance. The borrower is responsible for making insurance arrangements and paying the costs of the insurance premiums directly to the insurance company. A copy of the insurance policy showing the lender is on the policy as being paid first or second, as the case may be, has to be provided to the lender's lawyer before any mortgage funds are advanced. The insurance you carry covers only fire damage to the *inside* of your unit. The condominium corporation will have fire insurance coverage for damage to the *outside* of your unit. This premium would be included in your monthly maintenance fee. Refer to the discussion in chapter 5 on insurance.

Contribution to Property Tax Account

Many lenders require that you pay 1/12 of the projected annual taxes each month. This payment would be built into your monthly mortgage obligations, and the lender would set up a separate tax account and remit the taxes directly to the municipality at the appropriate time each year. Normally taxes are payable in June or July every year although they are calculated on the calendar year, that is, January 1 to December 31. Some municipalities require an advance part-payment in February of each year and the balance in July of that year. If the lender makes the automatic monthly tax payment a condition of mortgage approval, make sure that you inquire as to whether interest is going to be paid on your tax account to your credit, and if so ask about the interest rate. The interest paid is normally lower than the interest paid on deposit accounts. The reason why some lenders require monthly payments is to minimize the risk that you will not have sufficient funds to pay the taxes every year; if this happened, the property could conceivably be put up for tax sale and jeopardize the lender's security.

In most cases, the lender will give you the option to be responsible for paying your own taxes directly once a year. Make sure you request this. If you are paying a portion of the projected property tax every month, you will have to build that expense into the costs related to your mortgage.

Property Tax Adjustment Holdback

This concept is related to the previous topic. If the lender requires that you pay a portion of the property taxes every month, and if you purchase the condominium on April 1 with property taxes due in July, obviously there will be a shortfall in the tax account. In other words, if the property taxes are due and payable in full on July 1, and you have made payments each month of 1/12 of the projected annual tax, then by July 1 the tax account set up by the lender will be short by 9/12 of the amount required to pay the taxes.

The lender may require that you pay 9/12 of the projected annual tax into the tax account at the time of closing of the mortgage transaction. Either you would have to come up with these funds additionally or the lender would subtract that amount of money from the mortgage proceeds being made available to you. Alternatively you may be required to pay 4/12 of the projected property tax to the lender for each of the three months of April, May, and June prior to the tax payment deadline of July 1.

Interest Adjustment

When you pay rent you are paying in advance. When you pay mortgage payments to the lender for principal and interest, you are paying in arrears. In other words, if you make a mortgage payment on March 1, it is to cover the use of the funds and the interest on those funds for the month of February.

Because the lender's internal system is geared to a monthly payment basis, assuming that it is a fixed interest rate, the lender will want to be paid in advance for the use of the funds from February 15 until March 1. This interest adjustment is then advanced from the mortgage funds provided to you on February 15 so that the interest is pre-paid up to March 1. When your normal mortgage payment would be made on April 1, it would cover the one-month interest for the month of March plus a small repayment of the principal. Not all lenders require this arrangement, but you should know in advance so that you are aware of the net proceeds that you will receive on the mortgage.

Interest

Interest is of course a cost of having the funds paid to you under a mortgage. What you will have to pay for interest, and the steps you should go through to obtain the most attractive interest rate, have been discussed earlier in this chapter.

Provincial Mortgage Filing Fee

Most provinces charge a tax or a fee for filing a mortgage in the land registry.

Provincial Property Purchase Tax

Some provinces charge a fee based on a percentage of the value of the purchase.

Legal Fees and Disbursements

You are responsible for paying the lawyer for legal fees as well as out-of-pocket disbursements that the lawyer incurs relating to the preparation and filing of the mortgage documentation. Disbursements would cover such things as property searches, photocopy expenses, courier costs, and other costs associated with the preparation and registration of the mortgage. The disbursement costs would normally include the provincial mortgage filing tax or fee referred to above. It is the normal practice for lawyers to deduct the legal fees and disbursements directly from the money to be advanced under the mortgage. You will pay the GST on legal fees and disbursements. In some provinces, you pay PST on the legal fees as well.

Sometimes lenders require that you use a particular law firm, or you have the choice of which one of several law firms you would prefer to deal with. Other times the lender will permit you to use a lawyer of your choice. In all cases you are responsible for the legal fees and disbursements.

The Goods and Services Tax (GST)

The GST is covered in chapter 4.

Tip #35: Mortgage Life Insurance Premiums vs. Term Insurance

Mortgage life insurance is not the same as mortgage insurance. Many of the lending institutions provide an option for you to purchase insurance that will pay off the mortgage in the event of your death, the premium for which is generally included in your monthly payments. You should compare with term insurance from private insurance carriers to see if the rates are competitive. As an option you may prefer to protect yourself by taking out your own term insurance which would be payable to your estate in the event of your death; your estate would then have sufficient proceeds to pay off the mortgage. Another benefit of taking out term insurance is that it is portable, even if you are subsequently un-insurable due to health conditions. Finally, term insurance has the advantage of being a fixed and predictable amount, whereas the insurable amount of mortgage life insurance diminishes with every passing year—as you pay down the mortgage. You don't have this protection if you use lender mortgage life insurance. That is only applicable for the life of the mortgage. You may decide to use another lender in the future but are not eligible for that coverage anymore due to health conditions.

In certain circumstances a lender may require, as a condition of mortgage approval, that you take out the mortgage life insurance. This would normally only be in a situation where the lender felt your health to be a risk factor. Again, you could purchase your own term insurance or other type of life insurance and verify to the lender that you had such insurance. The lender may require that he be shown on the insurance policy as being paid first from the proceeds, but this would be an unusual type of request; it would be more likely if one were borrowing money through a mortgage for investment or commercial purposes.

Tip #36: Using the Money in Your RRSP

The Home Buyers Plan (HBP) allows you to withdraw up to $20,000 from your RRSP to buy or build a qualifying home. This is permitted under CRA policy. Two or more joint owners may use the HBP for the purchase of the same residence. Generally, you can participate in the HBP only once in your lifetime, as it is designed for first-time home buyers. Also, you need to occupy the home, not turn it into investment real estate and rent it out. However, you can have a "mortgage helper" suite rental of course.

You do not have to include the withdrawn amounts in your income, and the RRSP issuer will not withhold tax on these amounts.

Under the HBP, you have to repay the withdrawal to your RRSP within a period of not more than 15 years. Generally, you will have to repay a minimum amount to your RRSP each year, e.g., 1/15 of the withdrawn amount, until you have repaid the full amount you withdrew. If in any year you do not repay the amount you have to repay for that year, the amount you do not repay will be included in your taxable income for that year. Check with CRA for the current government policies. The website you will find in the Appendix.

Tip #37: What Your Options Are If You Default on Your Mortgage

As long as you meet the payments and the terms as agreed with the mortgage company, the mortgage company cannot commence any action to foreclose on the property. On the other hand, if you have difficulty with your payments or breach any terms of the mortgage, there are very severe remedies that the lender has available to protect its security. Defaulting on a mortgage has potentially serious consequences. If you are consistently late with your payments, this could affect your credit rating, and also your ability to renew your mortgage or obtain other mortgages in the future. This discussion will cover factors that constitute default, the mortgagor's options, and the mortgagee's options. It is not within the scope of this book to go into any more detail on mortgage default or foreclosure, other than to give an overview of the issues to consider.

Factors that Constitute Default under a Mortgage

The mortgage agreement sets out in considerable detail the requirements of the mortgagor. Some of these common clauses were discussed earlier. The main areas of default would be:

- failure to make your mortgage payments.
- failure to pay your taxes.
- failure to have insurance, or sufficient insurance.
- failure to obey municipal, provincial, or federal law as it relates to the premises that you have mortgaged.
- failure to maintain the premises in habitable condition.
- failure to keep the premises in proper repair.
- deliberately damaging the property that secures the mortgage.

Mortgage Borrower's Options on Default

If a borrower is having difficulty maintaining payments under the mortgage, there are many options to consider. You can:

- Make arrangements with the lender for a waiver of payments for a period of time (e.g., three or six months), or arrange for partial payments to be made. This is normally done in a situation where the borrower is sick, injured, or laid off, or has a reduced monthly income to debt-service the mortgage due to a marital separation, a spouse who has been laid off, or other such factors.

- Reschedule the debt and make new payment arrangements.

- Refinance the mortgage with another lender on terms that are more flexible and appropriate in the circumstances.

- Provide additional security to the lender in order to negotiate concessions.

- Put the property up for sale.

- Give the property back to the lender by means of quit claim (transfer of title to the lender) or a similar arrangement.

Exercise your right of redemption.

You are generally entitled to this by law. This means you pay the arrears outstanding under the mortgage, which prevents the mortgagee from commencing or from continuing foreclosure proceedings. An exception is that if there is an acceleration clause, which many mortgages have, the lender is entitled to deem the full amount of the mortgage immediately due and payable. In that event, you would have to pay the full amount of the mortgage in order to stop foreclosure proceedings. In most provinces you have a right of redemption of six months in order to pay the lender, or the lender would be entitled to take over the property, among other remedies.

Ask the court for more time.

If you can see that you are not able to pay off the lender within the six-month right of redemption period, you are entitled to request an extension from the court. The extension could be for an additional three months or six months or longer, and you are entitled to go back to the court to ask for further extensions. Whether the court grants an extension depends on the circumstances. For example, it is in your favour if you had previously lost your job and you are now employed, you are expecting proceeds from an inheritance, or you are having a family member raise funds for you. All these are factors that could show that the delay request is based on a realistic assessment of the ability to make the necessary payment. Having a substantial equity in the property would also assist you.

Tip #38: Options for the Lender on Default

If you are in default and despite all your efforts are unable to come to terms with the lenders, they have various options. Generally the last thing they want to do is take over the property, as there are other remedies that are more appropriate depending on the circumstances. The lenders are required to go to the court and get approval for most of the main remedies available. That gives you an opportunity to present your side of the situation and reveal unique circumstances if you wish.

Legislation governing the mortgage is provincial and there can be variation among the provinces. For the most part, though, the following remedies would be available to the lender:

Pay taxes, maintenance fees, or insurance premiums on your behalf.

The lender then adds these payments onto your total mortgage debt and charges interest on the amount.

Obtain an injunction from the court that you stop carrying on some improper or illegal activity.

In addition, the order could require you to perform some specific obligation under the mortgage document to protect the mortgage security. You would have to pay the lender's costs of obtaining the injunction.

Take possession of the premises to preserve the mortgage security.

This procedure is not often utilized except in serious situations involving revenue properties that are not properly being managed by the borrower.

Obtain a court order to put the property into receivership.

In this case, an independent party called a receiver-manager or receiver, takes possession of the property on behalf of the lender and maintains it. This procedure is rarely appropriate in a residential context, and is usually used only in the case of revenue property.

Accelerate the mortgage.

The lender has a choice of either requesting the arrears under the mortgage or deeming the full amount of the balance outstanding on the mortgage as immediately due and payable. The lender cannot request this latter course unless there is an acceleration clause in the mortgage. Some provinces do not permit acceleration clauses.

Sell the property.

This would mean that the lender would be able to put your property up for sale and sell it if you are in default in your payments over a set period of time. The period of time depends on the province. In many cases the lender will go through the court to get a court order to a sale so that the court can monitor the sale price and therefore minimize the risk that the borrower could claim that the house was undersold. In some provinces, the lender can activate an order for sale (in other words, require that the property be listed for sale) with 30 days' notice.

Sue the borrower personally for the debt outstanding.

The liability of the borrower under the terms of the mortgage remains an option for the lender whether or not the property has been sold. If it is sold, the borrower is responsible for any shortfall. The lender is not required to commence other actions such as foreclosure or sale of the property.

Foreclose against the property.

In a foreclosure situation, the lender requests that the court extinguish your rights of redemption and transfer all legal interest that you have, including the right of possession and legal title, to the lender. In this situation, the lender is entitled to all the equity in the property. The courts have to be involved in this procedure and your rights are protected in that regard. For example, the court would consider it inequitable if you had considerable equity in the property. It would probably advise the lender that instead of foreclosure there should be an order for sale. The purpose would be so that the equity in the mortgage property would be able to go to the mortgagor after all the costs associated with the sale, including sales commission, the lender's legal expenses, and disbursements, plus principal and interest outstanding, were paid off. Foreclosure actions as described above are not that common.

As you can see, there are many factors to consider if you are having financial difficulties on your mortgage. The circumstances of your default will make a difference in terms of what steps you wish to take. Contacting the lender and attempting to negotiate a resolution is clearly the first step that you should take to resolve the problem. If that does not turn out to be a satisfactory procedure, it would be prudent to obtain advice from a lawyer specializing in foreclosure matters so that you are fully aware of your available rights and options.

CHAPTER 4 — Purchasing Your Condo

This part will take you through all the key issues you need to consider when buying your condo. This includes understanding real estate cycles, selecting professionals, what features to look for in your condo, what due diligence research to do, looking at why a condo might be for sale (any negatives behind the purchase?), negotiating the price, typical closing costs to expect, and classic pitfalls to avoid.

Tip #39: Understanding What's Behind Real Estate Cycles

In order to have a better appreciation of how the real estate market operates, and how to operate prudently within that market, you need to understand the cycles and factors that influence prices and interest rates. No buying or selling decisions should be made without having conducted an accurate market assessment.

The Real Estate Cycle

Real estate is a cyclical industry. As in any such industry, the cycle historically creates shortage and excess. This relates to the issue of supply and demand in the marketplace. Too much supply creates a reduction in value. Too little supply creates an increase in value. It is essential to know where you are in the cycle relative to the exact location of your potential purchase. It is also important to understand that different provinces, regions, and communities are at different points of the economic cycle. Timing in the cycle is important when making buying or selling decisions.

One of the reasons for the cycle is that many developers are entrepreneurial by nature and operate primarily by short-term planning. If financing and

credit are available, developers tend to build without regard for the overall supply and demand. If a consequent glut occurs and the demand is slow, prices
come down as houses and condominiums go unsold.

Factors that play a role in real estate cycles include:

General Business Economic Cycles

The economy historically goes through periods of increased economic growth
followed by recessionary periods. The economic impact is greater, of course, in
certain parts of the country than in others in any given cycle. In a recessionary
period, people lose their jobs and have to put their houses on the market. Real
estate prices become depressed as potential purchasers decide to wait until the
economy is more secure.

It is difficult to know for certain when a recessionary economy will turn
around, but various indicators should give you some insight. If the economy
has been in a recession for a sustained period of time, there could be definite
opportunities to buy. Once the economy comes out of a recession, prices tend
to climb. Conversely, if the economy has been on a buoyant growth trend for
an extended period of time, be cautious in purchasing because a change in the
cycle, and therefore a drop in real estate prices, could be imminent.

Local Business Cycles

Each local economy has its own cycle and factors that impact on real estate
prices. These factors may not be greatly influenced by the general (provincial
or national) business cycles just discussed.

Community Cycles

Certain geographic locations within a community can have their own economic cycles as well as supply and demand status, all of which affect real estate
prices. In addition, a community has its own life cycle from growth to decline
to stagnation to rehabilitation. Look for areas of future growth.

As you can see, being aware of economic, business, and community cycles
is critical to prudent decision-making. Before buying or selling real estate in
a certain area, determine how these factors are impacting the cycle of the real

estate market. Different types of real estate—for example, condominiums, new houses, or resale houses—can be at different points of a cycle.

There are distinct segments to a real estate cycle. Each of these segments exhibits certain characteristics that are helpful cues in assessing the condition of the real estate market. For example, depending on where the market is on the cycle, the curve would show if the market is decreasing or increasing in value, plateauing, or declining. Some of the indicators you can look for include real estate values, rent levels, vacancy levels, occupancy levels, new construction starts, developers' profit margins, investor confidence, and nature of media coverage.

Tip #40: Identifying the Three Types of Real Estate Markets

You are probably familiar with the terminology used to describe the three types of real estate markets. As a brief review, they are:

Seller's Market

In a seller's market, the number of buyers wanting homes, for example, exceeds the supply or number of homes on the market. This type of market is characterized by homes that sell quickly, an increase in prices, a large number of buyers, and a minimal inventory of homes. These characteristics have implications for the buyer who has to make decisions quickly, must pay more, and frequently has his conditional offers rejected.

Buyer's Market

In a buyer's market, the supply of homes on the market exceeds the demand or number of buyers. Homes will remain in the market longer, there are fewer buyers for available properties, the inventory of homes grows, and prices fall. The implications for buyers in this type of market are more favorable negotiating leverage, more time to search for a home, and better prices.

Balanced Market

In a balanced market, the number of homes on the market is equal to the demand or number of buyers. Houses will sell within a reasonable period, demand equals supply, sellers accept reasonable offers, and prices are generally stabilized. The implications for the buyer of this type of market are that the atmosphere is still somewhat relaxed and there are a reasonable number of homes from which to choose.

Tip #41: Identifying Factors that Affect Prices

There are many factors that influence the price of real estate. Whether you are a buyer or seller, you need to understand what factors are present that are impacting on the market, so you can make the right decisions at the right time and in the right location. Many of these factors are interconnected.

Position in Real Estate Cycle

As described earlier, the position of the particular real estate market in the cycle will have a bearing on prices.

Interest Rates

There is a direct connection between interest rates and prices. The higher the rates, the lower the prices. The lower the rates, the higher the prices. The lower the rates, the more people can afford to buy their first home or an investment property. This puts pressure or greater demand on the market. Interest rates will be discussed further.

Taxes

An area where municipal property taxes are high can be a disincentive to a purchaser. This could cause the real estate prices to drop. Provincial taxes, such as a property purchase tax, will put some buyers off. Federal tax legislation on real estate, such as changes in capital gains tax, could have a negative influence on investors. All these factors would affect the overall amount of real estate activity, including prices.

Rent Controls

Naturally, provincial rent controls and related restrictions could have a limiting effect on investor real estate activity, thereby resulting in fewer buyers in the market for certain types of homes.

Local Economy

Confidence in the economy can stimulate home buyer and investor activity. If the economy is buoyant and the mood is positive, more market activity will occur, generally resulting in a price increase. Conversely, if the economy is stagnant, the opposite dynamic occurs, resulting in a decrease in activity and lower prices. If real estate purchasers are concerned about the same problem, a predictable loss of confidence occurs in the market.

Population Shifts

A city or town with business, employment, tourism, and retirement opportunities will attract people who are new to Canada as well as people from other parts of the country. The increased demand will increase prices. Conversely, if there is net migration from the area due to plant closures, for example, environmental problems, or other factors, the opposite effect on real estate prices will occur, forcing them to go down.

Vacancy Levels

If there are high vacancy levels, this could reduce investor confidence due to the potential risk of not finding a tenant, and real estate sales could go down. On the other hand, if there are low vacancy levels, this could stimulate investor activity as well as those entering the market for the first time.

Location

This is an important factor. Highly desirable locations will generally go up in price more quickly and consistently. Property that offers a stunning view tends to escalate the most, for obvious reasons. Waterfront property is desirable due to its limited supply and high demand.

Availability of Land

If there is a natural shortage of land, municipal zoning restrictions, limits on development or provincial land use laws that restrict the utilization of existing land for housing purposes, this will generally cause prices to increase. Again, it relates back to the principle of supply and demand.

Public Image

The perception by the public of a certain geographic location or type of residential property or builder will affect demand and, therefore, price. Some areas or types of properties are "hot" and some are not at any given time.

Political Factors

The policy of a provincial or municipal government in terms of supporting real estate development will naturally have a positive or negative effect on supply and demand and therefore prices.

Seasonal Factors

Certain times of year are traditionally slow months for residential real estate sales (November through February and sometimes March, depending on the weather), hence prices decline. The same seasonal factor impacts on recreational property.

The Baby Boom Generation

The boomer generation has a dramatic impact on the real estate market. With boomers inheriting trillions of dollars—a trend that will last 10 to 15 more years—there will be considerable disposable income to buy investment real estate. Many boomers are buying and want to buy recreational property for lifestyle balance, quality of life, and to have a central place for the extended or blended family to congregate. In addition, many boomers are downsizing and buying condos, to enable them to maintain an active lifestyle, provide a sense of security and feeling of community, and enable freedom from house maintenance.

Tip #42: Assemble Your Team: How to Find the Right Realtor

When buying real estate, whether you are purchasing a principal residence or an investment property, it is essential to have a team of experts and professionals to assist you in achieving your goals. They will provide peace of mind and help you avoid pitfalls and protect your investment. Depending on your needs, the team could consist of a realtor, lawyer, accountant, mortgage broker (covered in chapter 3), building inspector, and insurance broker. (You will find websites to locate the above advisors and professionals by referring to the Helpful Websites section of the Appendix. Note that "Selecting a Lawyer" is discussed in detail in chapter 5.)

Selecting a Realtor

There are distinct advantages to having a realtor acting for you in buying or selling a property. As in any profession, there is a range of competence among licensed real estate salespeople throughout Canada. However, with careful selection you can minimize the risk and benefit greatly from the skills of a knowledgeable, experienced, and sincere realtor.

There are many ways to select a realtor. Here are some suggestions. The reality is that over 70% of buyers use the Internet as a primary initial search vehicle to research and short-list properties of interest. The potential buyer can go directly to the listing broker, or use their own broker to follow up.

Locating a Realtor

There are a number of approaches to finding a good real estate agent:

- Ask friends, neighbours, and relatives for the names of agents they know and would recommend.

- Open houses provide an opportunity to meet realtors.

- Newspaper ads list the names and phone numbers of agents who are active in your area.

- Search the Internet for realtors in the locale you are considering to buy in.

- "For Sale" signs provide an agent's name and phone number.

- Real estate firms in your area can be contacted; speak to an agent who specializes or deals with the type of property you want, e.g., condos, and is an experienced salesperson and familiar with the geographic area and community that interests you.

After you have met several agents who could potentially meet your needs, there are a number of guidelines to assist you with your selection:

- Favour an agent who is familiar with the neighbourhood in which you are interested. Such an agent will be on top of the available listings, will know comparable market prices, and can target the types of property that meet your needs as you have explained them.

- Favour an agent who is particularly familiar with the buying and selling of condominiums.

- Favour an agent who is experienced and knowledgeable in the real estate industry.

- Look for an agent who is prepared to pre-screen properties so that you are informed only of those that conform to your guidelines for viewing purposes.

- Look for an agent who is familiar with the various conventional and creative methods of financing, including the effective use of mortgage brokers.

- Look for an agent who is thorough on the type of properties you are keen on, in terms of background information such as length of time on the market, reason for sale, and price comparisons among similar properties. An agent can use the additional resources available on their Multiple Listing Service (MLS) computer to find out a great amount of additional information in a short time, assuming the property is listed on the MLS. For example, length of time on the market and any price increases or decreases, comparisons with other condos' recent sales or asking prices in the same building, condo project, or neighbourhood, etc.

- Look for an agent who will be candid with you in suggesting a real estate offer price and explain the reasons for the recommendation.

- Look for an agent who has effective negotiating skills to ensure that your wishes are presented as clearly and persuasively as possible.

- Favour an agent who is working on a full-time basis, not dabbling part-time.

- Look for an agent who attempts to upgrade his professional skills and expertise.

- Look for an agent who is good with numbers, in other words is familiar with the use of financial calculations. This is particularly important if you are buying revenue property.

- Because of the amount of time the agent will be spending on your behalf, you should give the agent your exclusive business if you have confidence in him or her. You want to keep the agent motivated. Keep the agent informed of any open houses in which you are interested. Advise any other agents that you have one working for you. Focus clearly on your needs and provide the agent with a written outline of your specific criteria to assist in short-listing potential prospects. If for any reason you are dissatisfied with the agent who is assisting you, find another as quickly as possible.

Benefits to the Purchaser

There are obvious benefits to the buyer of using a realtor as outlined in the previous points. One of the key benefits is that the realtor can act as an intermediary between you and the listing broker. That way, the listing broker may never have an opportunity to meet you, and therefore cannot exert any influence on you with persuasive salesmanship, or otherwise make an assessment of you and your emotions or motivation that could compromise your negotiating position.

The agent who has the listing agreement with the vendor would only know you through discussions with the realtor with whom you are dealing and through any offer that you might present. This "arm's length" negotiating position is an important strategic tactic that will be of benefit to you.

You should know about the concept of a "buyer broker." This is a licensed agent who will represent your interests exclusively. This is confirmed in writing and the listing broker is informed of this. The buyer broker still gets the commission cut from the sale, so you don't have to pay him anything. If you don't have a buyer broker relationship in writing, the listing broker has the primary duty to the vendor, and the broker whom you otherwise use is technically a sub-agent of the listing broker. In both these scenarios, the agents legally represent the interests of the vendor.

In many cases, realtors can refer you to a lender or mortgage broker to assist you in arranging mortgage financing. However, as discussed previously, you are further ahead by using a mortgage broker in most cases, as they are comparing the competitive lending market at a specific time, in terms of who is offering the best deal.

Tip #43: Assemble Your Team: How to Find the Right Accountant

If you are considering a condominium purchase as an investment in real estate, the right professional accountant will monitor the financial health of your investment and reduce the subsequent risks and tax payable. Along with your lawyer, your accountant will complement your real estate team to ensure that your real estate investment decisions are based on sound advice and good planning. Some accountants have also obtained their certified financial planner (CFP) certification, in order to offer their clients comprehensive consulting advice.

An accountant can help you even before you invest in real estate. The services that can be provided are wide-ranging and include the following:

- setting up a manual or computerized bookkeeping system that both the investor and accountant can work with efficiently.
- setting up a customized software program for real estate investment and management of the properties.

- setting up systems for the control of cash and the handling of funds.

- preparing or evaluating budgets, forecasts, and investment plans.

- assessing your break-even point and improving your profitability.

- preparing and interpreting financial statements.

- providing tax- and financial-planning advice.

- preparing corporate and individual tax returns.

In Canada, anyone can call himself an accountant. One can also adopt the title "public accountant" without any qualifications, experience, regulations, or accountability to a professional association. That is why you have to be very careful when selecting the appropriate accountant for your needs. There are three main designations of qualified professional accountants in Canada: chartered accountant (CA), certified general accountant (CGA), and certified management accountant (CMA). Accountants with the above designations are governed by provincial statutes. The conduct, professional standards, training, qualifications, professional development, and discipline of these professionals are regulated by their respective institutes or associations. Rely on the advice of an accountant, therefore, only after you have satisfied yourself that the accountant meets the professional qualifications that you require for your real estate investment needs.

How to Find an Accountant

Referrals

Often a banker, lawyer, or other business associate will be pleased to recommend an accountant who has expertise in real estate investment. Such referrals are valuable since these individuals are probably aware of your area of interest and would recommend an accountant only if they felt he or she was well qualified and had a good track record in assisting real estate investors.

Professional Associations

The professional institutes that govern CAs, CGAs, and CMAs may be a source of leads. You can telephone or write the institute or association with a request for the names of three accountants who provide public accounting services to real estate investors within your geographic area. Also, check out provincial association websites. Refer to the Appendix for contact sites. Often an initial consultation is free of charge. Always find out before you confirm the appointment.

Yellow Pages

In the Yellow Pages, under the heading "Accountants," you will find listings under the categories "Chartered," "Registered," "Certified General," and "Management."

Searching the Internet

Do a Google search (www.google.ca).

Tip #44: Assemble Your Team: How to Find the Right Home Inspector

One of the most important aspects of purchasing your principal residence or investment property is to know the condition of the property in advance. You don't want to have problems after you buy that will cost you money to repair. You could lose all your potential profit on sale, and put your investment at risk otherwise.

Make sure when you obtain an inspection that the person doing it is qualified and independent. Ask what association he or she belongs to, if any, and, if not, why not. One of the larger associations in Canada is the Canadian Association of Home and Property Inspectors (CAHPI), which has various provincial chapters. (Refer to the Appendix for the website under Helpful Websites.) To become a member of CAHPI, an inspector must meet various professional and educational requirements, successfully complete a training course and write exams, and practise professionally for a trial period before being considered by the association. In addition, there are annual continuing education requirements to ensure that inspectors keep their industry knowledge current.

Services Provided by a Home Inspector

A home inspector is an objective expert who examines the home and gives you a written opinion of its condition and, ideally, the approximate range of costs to repair the problems. Home inspectors look at all the key parts of the building, such as condition of the roof, siding, foundation, basement, flooring, walls, windows, doors, garage, drainage, electrical, heating, cooling, ventilation, plumbing, insulation, and so on. They should also look for signs of wood rot, mould, and insects.

The older the building, the more potential problems, but new buildings can have serious problems as well. If the new building is covered by a New Home Warranty Program, then you have some protection. However, that program does have some exclusions, and you don't need the hassle of rectifying a problem. If a new home is not covered by the New Home Warranty Program, or is not a new property, you definitely want a home inspection; otherwise, you might have to pay to repair the problem if the builder refuses to do so or goes out of business. You can have an inspection done of a townhouse, or apartment condominium, or any type of residential type of building.

Quite apart from avoiding expensive surprises, using a home inspector has another potential benefit. If the report shows problems with a quantifiable cost to rectify it, you could use that information to negotiate a reduction in the property's price to reflect the estimated cost of repair. You may not want to buy the home, even if problems can be rectified. At least the report gives some objective professional's opinion on the condition of the home to discuss with the vendor.

Make sure that you put a condition in your offer that says "subject to purchaser obtaining a home inspection satisfactory to the purchaser within X days of acceptance of the offer." This way it will be at your discretion whether you want to complete the deal or not. In addition to the need for a home inspection, you might also be able to obtain a "vendor's disclosure statement." Real estate boards in some provinces have prepared such a form for vendors to sign, disclosing any known problems with the home. As this is a voluntary program in many cases, ask for the reasons if a vendor refuses to complete the form. Have a professional home inspection done anyway, for obvious reasons. The owner may honestly not be aware of serious problems with the home if they are not visible or obvious.

How to Select a Home Inspector

It is important to obtain a qualified and independent inspector. Avoid someone who has a contractor business on the side and may hope to get the repair business from you. Their advice could be self-serving and biased. Apply the same selection criteria discussed earlier in this chapter. Look in the Yellow Pages of your telephone directory under "Building Inspection Services." You can also ask friends, relatives, neighbours, or your real estate agent for names of inspection companies they know and recommend. Call several inspectors in your area and interview them. Check with your local Better Business Bureau to see if there have been any complaints against the company that you are considering. Ask for references and check out the references.

Home inspection fees range from approximately $200 to $400 or more, depending on the expertise required and the nature of the inspection, the size of the home, its age and condition, your geographic area, the nature of inspection services requested, and other variables. It normally takes a minimum of three hours to do a thorough inspection.

Questions to Ask

Here are the questions that you should ask when deciding which inspection company to select:

- What does the inspection include? Always make sure that you get a written report and ask for a sample of a report and what will be covered.

- How much will it cost? Determine the fees up front.

- How long will the inspection take?

- Does the inspector encourage the client to attend the inspection? This is a valuable educational opportunity. You will have a chance to see the problems first-hand. You will also learn various helpful maintenance tips. If an inspector refuses to have you attend the inspection, this should raise a red flag.

- How long has the inspector been in the business as a home inspection firm and what type of work was the inspector doing before inspecting homes?

- Is the inspector specifically experienced in residential construction?

- What and where was the inspector's training? Does the inspector participate in continuing education programs to keep his or her expertise up to date?

- Does the company offer to do any repairs or improvements based on its inspection? This might cause a conflict of interest.

- Does the inspector carry errors and omission insurance? This means that if the inspector makes a mistake in the inspection and you have to pay to rectify the problem, the insurance will cover it. How much insurance does the inspector have and are there any restrictions or exceptions? Can you have a copy to review? Will the inspector confirm all that in writing before you make a decision to have the inspection done?

- Does the inspector belong to an association that will investigate any consumer complaint?

- What percentage of time does the inspector deal with condos?

Tip #45: Assemble Your Team: How to Find the Right Insurance Broker

An insurance broker is not committed to any particular company and therefore can compare and contrast the different policies, coverage, and premiums from a wide range of companies that relate to the type of insurance coverage that you are looking for. Also, insurance brokers can obtain a premium quotation for you and coverage availability from insurance company underwriters if the particular investment you have is unique or difficult to cover by other existing policies. Insurance brokers generally have a wide range of types of insurance available. Ensure that the broker is affiliated with a reputable firm.

Every type of lender for real estate requires insurance. Creditors such as banks often require insurance. The main categories and types of insurance that you should consider and discuss with your insurance broker are discussed in chapter 5.

How to Find an Insurance Broker

There are several ways to find an insurance broker:

- Look in the Yellow Pages under "Insurance Brokers."
- Ask your accountant, lawyer, business associates, and friends for a recommendation.
- Search the Internet.
- Check with the Insurance Brokers Association of Canada (www.ibac.ca) for names of members in your area.

Tip #46: The Essential Factors of Buying a Condominium

Certain factors may be more or less important, depending on whether you are buying a condo for personal use (principal residence) or as an investment.

Location

One of the prime considerations is the location. How close is the property to schools, cultural attractions, shopping centres, recreational facilities, work, and transportation? How attractive is the present and future development of the area surrounding the property? You could buy a condo and six months later a shopping complex could be built across the street, blocking your view and therefore decreasing the resale value of your property. The location should have ample access to parking and other attractive features. Check on the amount of traffic on the streets in your area. Heavy traffic can be a noise nuisance as well as a hazard for young children.

Noise

As best you can, assess the levels of noise. Consider such factors as nearby highways or busy streets, driveways, parking lots, playgrounds, and businesses. When buying a condominium, it is particularly important to consider the location of the garage doors, elevators, garbage chutes, and the heating and air-conditioning plant or equipment.

Privacy

Privacy is an important consideration and has to be thoroughly explored. For example, you want to make sure that the sound insulation between the walls, floors, and ceilings of your property is sufficient to enable you to live comfortably without annoying your neighbours or having your neighbours annoy you. Such factors as the distance between your unit and other common areas, including walkways, roads, and fences, are important.

Pricing

The pricing of the property you are considering should be competitive with that of other, similar offerings. On the other hand, when purchasing a condominium unit, it is sometimes difficult to compare prices accurately without taking into account the different amenities that may be available in one condominium that are not available in another—for example, tennis courts, swimming pool, recreation centre, etc. You may decide that you do not want these extra facilities in view of your lifestyle needs, in which case paying an extra price for the unit because of these features would not be economical. On the other hand, you have to look at the resale potential, so check with your realtor. He or she can obtain accurate information on comparative pricing and cost per square foot for similar properties in the same condo building or complex.

Common Elements and Facilities

When buying a condominium unit, review all the common elements that make up the condominium development. Consider these from the perspective of the relevance to your needs as well as the maintenance or operational costs that might be required to service these features.

Parking Facilities

Are the facilities outdoors or underground? Do you feel there is sufficient lighting for security protection? Is it a long distance from the parking spot to your home? Is there parking space available for a boat, trailer, or second car, and is there ample visitor parking?

Storage Facilities

Check out the type of storage space available, including location and size. Does there appear to be sufficient storage space for your needs, or will you have to rent a mini-locker to store excess items?

Quality of Construction Materials

Thoroughly look at your building and the surrounding development in an attempt to make an assessment of the overall quality of the development. Keep in mind that you will be responsible for paying a portion of the maintenance costs for the common elements. You may wish to hire a contractor whom you trust, or a building inspector, to give you an opinion on the quality and condition of the building or unit before committing yourself. An older building is clearly going to cost money to repair, and possibly in a short period of time.

Design and Layout

When looking at a building, consider your present and future needs. In a condominium, although you are entitled to use the interior of your unit as you wish, there are restrictions relating to the exterior of your unit or any structural changes that you may make to the unit. If you are intending to have a separate room for an expanded family, in-laws, or an office, you should consider the implications beforehand. For example, you may find that the balcony is very windy and you would like to have a solarium built to enclose the balcony for that reason. There is a very good chance that you would not be able to do so without the consent of the condominium council, because it would affect the exterior appearance of the development.

Neighbourhood

Look at the surrounding neighbourhood and make an assessment as to whether the value of the residences in the neighbourhood will affect the value of your property. For example, are the buildings and homes in the area well maintained? Are there children in the same age group as your own children? Is the neighbourhood characterized by single adults, young couples (with or without children), or older and retired people? Does your condo development permit children?

Owner/Occupiers vs. Tenants

Ask how many tenants as opposed to owners there are currently in the condominium complex, and the maximum number of tenants allowed. The higher the percentage of owner/occupiers, the better the chance that there will be more pride of ownership and, therefore, more responsible treatment of common elements and amenities. Generally speaking, you should be concerned if the tenant percentage in the condominium complex or residential area is 25% or more and is increasing, or does not have a rental cap. Of course, if you are buying a condo for investment purposes, you would be looking at matters from a different perspective.

Management

Inquire as to whether the condo building is being operated by a professional management company, operated by a resident manager, or is self-managed. Ideally, you should check out the condominium unit or property that you are interested in at three different times before you decide to purchase: during the day, in the evening, and on a weekend. That should give you a better profile of noise factors, children, or parties, and the effectiveness of the management control.

Property Taxes

Compare the costs of taxes in the area that you are considering with those of other areas equally attractive to you. Different municipalities have different tax rates and there could be a considerable cost saving or expense. Also inquire as to whether there is any anticipated tax increase and why.

Rental Situation in Area

Look for an area that enjoys a high rental demand if you are considering a condominium purchase as a revenue property. You want to minimize the risk of having a vacancy. Check with your realtor and various ongoing surveys to obtain average house and condominium rentals in the area. For example, many real estate companies and CMHC have free surveys on a quarterly or monthly basis, giving average rental prices in specific areas for specific types of properties. Refer to the Appendix under Helpful Websites for contact information. You don't want too high a number of rental houses or condos, as that will increase competition and possibly reduce the overall desirability of the neighbourhood.

Local Restrictions and Opportunities

Check to see what restrictions on use and other matters may exist. For example, is there a community plan? What type of bylaw zoning is there, and is it changing? Is there a rezoning potential for higher or different use? Is there a land use contract? What about non-conforming use of older or revenue buildings?

Image of the Area

What image does the media or the public in general have about a certain area? Is it positive or negative, and why? The perception of people as to the image of the area may have an effect on rental or purchase decisions.

Stage of Development

A community will typically go through a series of stages, phases, and plateaus over time. For example, the normal stages are development (growth), stabilization (maturing, plateau), conversions (from apartment to condos), improvements of existing properties, decline of improvements (deterioration), and redevelopment (tearing down of older buildings and new construction, more efficient use of space).

Economic Climate

This is a major factor to consider. What is stimulating the economy, and why is the community appealing to renters and home buyers? Are developments such as shopping centres, house and condo construction, office buildings, franchise outlets, and other commercial activity on the rise? Are there subways or other new public transportation plans proximate to the area in the making? Is the provincial or federal government going to construct or move offices to the community? Or is a major single-industry employer the main cause of economic activity in the area? In the latter case, you can appreciate the risk involved if the industry or main employer has financial problems or decides to close down or move away. Conversely, in many major centres, the commercial rent in downtown areas is high, and the commuting time and/or downtown residential rents or house prices inhibit employee retention. For this reason, many companies are moving their operations to suburbs where the commuting, rent, and cost of land is cheaper, and finding employees who appreciate lower housing costs is easier.

Population Trends

Look for the trends in the community you are considering. Are people moving in or out, and why? What is the average age? Type of employment? Income level? Family size? Many of these demographic statistics can be obtained from Statistics Canada or from your provincial or municipal government. If the population is increasing, it will generally create more demand for rental and resale housing. Conversely, if it is decreasing, the opposite will occur. If the population is of an older age group, people may prefer downsizing to condominiums rather than buying smaller houses. There are many variables to consider.

Transportation

You will want to have convenient transportation routes. Whether it is a bus, subway, rapid transit, freeway, ferry, or other mode of transportation, the quality of transportation will have a bearing on your lifestyle and future potential resale.

Appearance

Look at the appearance of the property you are interested in. Would it be attractive to someone else on resale? Is it well maintained, or does it need repair? What do the other buildings look like in the neighbourhood? Are they new, renovated, or attractive to look at? Or are they poorly maintained with paint peeling, grass uncut, windows broken, or garbage visible?

Services in the Community

Different services available in the community will attract different types of tenants or purchasers, depending on their needs—for example, shopping, churches, community and recreational facilities, playgrounds or parks, and schools.

Unattractive Features

Look for factors that will have a negative impact on a decision to purchase, for example, unpleasant odours coming from an industrial plant, poor lighting because of too many trees, lack of street lighting that impairs safety, inadequate municipal services such as septic tanks rather than sewer facilities, impaired roads, open drainage ditches, etc.

Convenient Proximity

If you are buying a condo as an investment, it is prudent to purchase within a four-hour-drive radius of your principal residence. This is just a general guide-line, of course. The point is that you want to be able to conveniently monitor and/or maintain your property.

Tip #47: Know the Real Reason Behind the Listing

An important factor to know is why a condo is up for sale. Perhaps the vendor knows something you don't, which will have a bearing on your further interest.

If you can, try to determine the real motivation for the owner to sell the condo. Try to dig below the surface. This will assist you in knowing how to negotiate in terms of your offer price and terms and general strategies. The motivation for sale could be a positive or negative one.

If you are interested in buying a condo for investment purposes, refer to my book for a discussion of the reasons why an investment condo could be for sale, and other helpful strategies when investing in real estate. The book is: *Making Money in Real Estate: The Canadian Guide to Profitable Investment in Residential Property*, 2nd edition, published by John Wiley & Sons. Also, check out the website www.homebuyer.ca for more information.

Some of the frequent reasons for sale of a principal residence include the following:

- Separation or divorce.

- Death of owner or co-owner.

- Loss of job of principal wage earner or of one of two wage earners when two wage earners are necessary to pay for the home expenses.

- Job relocation.

- Ill health of one or both homeowners.

- Retirement and therefore relocation or downsizing house-size needs, or desire to take some of the equity out of the condo for retirement purposes.

- Owner lost money in a business or other investment venture and needs to sell the condo to pay off the debt.

- Owner has not made payments on the mortgage due to personal or financial problems, so the lender has started court proceedings to have the condo sold.

- Owner wants to sell in a seller's market.

- Owner is concerned that the market is changing and could become a buyer's market.

- Owner is testing the market to see what the market will pay without making any serious attempt to sell.

- Children are leaving the home and therefore the owner's housing needs are changing.

- Owner wants to buy a larger home due to increasing family size or needs. This could also be due to having an extended family, e.g., in-law suite or extra space for parents or relatives, or blended family due to a second marriage or common-law relationship, etc.

- Owner wants to trade up to a nicer home or better neighbourhood.

- Owner wants to buy a house with a rental suite in basement for revenue purposes.

- Owner is trying to avoid an upcoming expensive special assessment for condo repairs (e.g., roof, leaking buildings) and/or major amenity upgrades and maintenance (e.g., pool).

- Owner is concerned the mix of renters and owner/occupiers is too high, and causing a negative impact on the condo community.

- Owner has a noisy neighbour or is facing a noisy street.

- Owner knows that a building development has been approved that will block the view from the condo.

Tip #48: Where to Look for Your Condo

There are some preliminary considerations you need to work through before starting your search.

General Guidelines

- Clearly define your needs and wants and why.

- Be clearly focused on what type of condominium you want and its location, in order to save time and stress.

- Do your preliminary research on the Internet through www.mls.ca and www.google.ca using keyword searches.

- Target a specific geographic area or areas. This means restricting your choices to specific communities or areas within a community. This makes your selection much easier and gives you an opportunity to get to know specific areas thoroughly. Obtain street maps of the area as well as a zoning map from city hall. You can also access detailed maps on the Internet through www.google.ca and www.mapquest.com.

- Know the price range that you want based on your available financing and real estate needs. Obtain a pre-approved mortgage so that you have that reality check.

- Determine the type of ideal purchase package that you want (e.g., price and terms) as well as your "bottom line" fallback position. You want to know the maximum you are willing to pay and the most restrictive terms that you can live with. Make sure that you don't compromise your own position.

- Do comparisons and short-list choices. That way you can ensure you get the best deal, in comparative terms.

- Be realistic in terms of your purchase conditions in light with the current market situation. Many people fantasize about buying real estate for less than the fair market value and keep searching for this elusive purchase. The reality is, that situation could be very difficult to find.

- Don't necessarily wait for mortgage rates to go down before looking. Higher mortgage rates generally mean less demand in the market and therefore lower prices and more negotiating leverage for the purchaser. Conversely, lower mortgage rates generally mean more demand in the market, and therefore higher prices and less negotiating leverage for the purchaser. These are guidelines only. The key factor is to buy at the right price, taking all the factors outlined in this chapter and other chapters into consideration. If mortgage rates come down, you can renegotiate a lower mortgage rate with or without a penalty, depending on the mortgage you originally negotiated.

- Remember, the location of a property is very important, especially for a principal residence. Location is, of course, also important for investment property, but it has to be balanced against overall investment goals such as tax benefits, appreciation, resale potential, net revenue, and risk assessment.

Where to Find Real Estate for Sale

There are various methods of finding out about real estate for sale. Here are some of the most common approaches.

Internet

As noted earlier, this is the primary research tool for over 70% of Canadians in locating a property of interest. There are many websites available. The

MLS site is a comprehensive listing at www.mls.ca. All the major real estate companies have their own websites with listings. Also do a keyword search on www.google.ca. Check out www.homebuyer.ca for helpful information.

Multiple Listing Service (MLS)

MLS is an excellent tool for obtaining condo listing information. If you are looking at an MLS book or online at www.mls.ca, look for specific factors that will give you clues as to vendor motivation. This could assist you in negotiating a lower price. For example, look for the exact area, when the property was listed (how long), if it has been re-listed, whether the property is vacant, if any price reductions have occurred (for how much and when), and whether there has been a previous collapsed sale. Also look in the remarks/comments section in the MLS listing book. For example, it could say why the property is for sale, such as foreclosure action, order for sale, relocation, bought another property, etc. All this information is important research for you. If you can't readily access any of the above information, ask your realtor for it.

Real Estate Agent

A good real estate agent is an invaluable asset for buying or selling real estate. He or she can save you time, expense, and frustration, and provide advice and expertise. Remember that the vendor pays the real estate commission whether the agent is a listing or selling broker.

There are many advantages to using realtors, which are discussed throughout this book. You can use their services to source out property listed on multiple or exclusive listings, or for property "for sale by owner." You can also use them to contact owners of property who do not currently have the property for sale. The advantage of using realtors with non-listed property is that they can possibly negotiate a better deal for you than you may be able to get yourself. There are strategic benefits to having an agent present the offer and negotiate on your behalf. Frequently, the owner will agree to pay a commission to the realtor if you buy, although the commission in a non-listed sale would generally be less. This is because the realtor has not had the expense of time or advertising in actively promoting the listing. Alternatively, you could arrange to pay the realtor a negotiated fee if he or she arranged a sale at a price attractive to you.

If you use a realtor to assist your search, be loyal to them if you purchase the property. On the other hand, if the realtor is turning out to be unmotivated, then find another. Make sure you give your agent a list of your requirements so they can be precise in their search for you.

Newspaper Ads

Look in the classified section of your daily or community newspaper. The weekend section tends to have the most listings. The Monday classified section has the fewest number of listings. Because fewer people look in the Monday section, that could mean fewer potential buyers are paying attention and leaving more opportunity for you. Ignore the sales puffery. Many ads are designed to entice you with the impression the owner is anxious and therefore imply that you may be able to get a better price. This may or may not be the case. Pay particular attention to ads that may imply that an owner is under time pressure, such as "estate sale," "owner transferred," or "foreclosure sale." Also, look in the special real estate newspapers that are available free and come out weekly in many major Canadian cities.

Drive Through Neighbourhoods

As mentioned earlier, it is important to develop a familiarity with the area in which you are interested. Drive through the area on a regular basis and look for "For Sale" signs, both property listed with a realtor and "For Sale by Owner." Take down addresses, names, and telephone numbers.

Through Word of Mouth

You could let your friends, neighbours, relatives, or business associates know that you are looking to buy property, the type of property, and the location, in case they hear of someone who is thinking of selling or see a property for sale in their neighbourhood that might interest you.

Tip #49: Pros and Cons of Different Types of Condos

There are different cautions and approaches when dealing with different types of condo sales. Here is a very brief overview. This book emphasizes the wide range of ways that you can protect yourself through knowledge and due diligence research before you sign on the dotted line. In all cases, you want to have the assistance of a real estate lawyer to review all the documents and give you advice. It can frequently be a challenge for a layperson to interpret the implications of the fine print. (Refer to the Appendix for the Condo Buyer's Checklist.)

Buying a Resale Condo

When you buy a previously owned condo, you need to ensure you obtain all the necessary documents and information. (The key documents will be discussed in chapter 5.) Depending on your province and your condo corporation, there could be additional documents. You want to make your offer to purchase subject to your lawyer obtaining all the relevant documents to review and being satisfied with them. Make sure you give yourself and your lawyer sufficient time to review and understand the documents—e.g., a week to 10 days. There will be a lot to review, as there is a history to the condo. You also want to ensure you obtain a home inspection on the unit and the building to check on construction quality. Talk to the people who own condos in the complex. Speak to a condo corporation director and the property management company about any problems and the governance of the condo corporation.

You want to ask detailed questions about the reserve/contingency fund, and what major expenses could be anticipated and when. You also want to review the annual report and read the last 24 months of condo corporation minutes to owners, to see if there are any matters of concern, e.g., leaking roofs, break-ins of cars and units, litigation pending, etc. If you are serious about buying a unit, it would be prudent to hire a competing condo property management company to the one used by your condo corporation, e.g., one of the larger and more experienced companies, to review the documentation and give you their candid feedback. They may have heard information that would either affirm it is a good location and complex, or one to stay away from. It would be inexpensive to obtain this third-party feedback—probably only $200 or so. That is money well spent. You want to see in the documents what the restrictions are on the total number of rental units that can be permitted in the complex.

Some of the **advantages** of buying a resale condo include:

- No lengthy wait time before you can move in.
- You can see what you are buying.
- There is a history to the complex in terms of operation and structure and any problems.
- You can speak to people who live in the complex to see if the community is a good fit for your lifestyle, needs, and wants.
- Condo developments that are older may have larger-sized units.
- There is no GST.
- Deposits tend to be lower.

Some of the **disadvantages** include:

- Major repairs could soon be required or planned for. If the reserve/contingency fund is insufficient, a special assessment could be charged to the owners to fund the repairs.
- Different construction standards could create problems with leaks, squeaks, noise, or heat loss.
- Older condo complexes tend to require more maintenance and therefore costs.
- The New Home Warranty coverage would likely have expired.
- Limited choice in types of units or upgrade potential.
- May lack in the amenities that are important to you.

Buying a Conversion Condo

This format means that the building was originally used for some other purpose but has been renovated for residential use. It could have been a rental apartment block before. Or if it is a loft-style condo, it could have been converted from a former industrial or commercial building. You would normally be buying this type of condo from the developer if it has just been converted. The same cautions and suggestions outlined for resale and new condos apply.

Some of the **advantages** of a conversion condo include:

- Possible creative and unique designs and layout.

- Tend to be less expensive than a new completed unit due to less core construction costs.

- Tend to be located in downtown areas of a city.

Some of the **disadvantages** include:

- As in a new-construction condo, the dates you have planned for occupancy could be delayed due to construction delays.

- If the core building is old, that could mean potential costly repair or maintenance costs in the future. Without an adequate contingency/reserve fund, that would mean that special assessments would be raised from condo owners.

- New Home Warranty coverage may not apply. For example, in a new construction the warranty company knows the quality of the construction and the builder. Dealing with a conversion of an older building has inherent risks for any New Home Warranty insurer. The developer could provide warranty coverage, but that is highly risky, as the developer could go under, or could have set up a corporation for the conversion that has no extra assets in it once the units have all been sold.

Buying a New Condo

If you are buying a new condo, there are additional cautions, as there is no history. That is, no history in terms of problems with the project. The term *new* refers to condo buildings that are under construction or recently completed. You want to make sure you obtain a home inspection anyway, even though it is new. You also want to check into New Home Warranty protection coverage. Do your due diligence on the reputation and experience of the developer. What other projects have they done? How long have they been in business? Can you check out a project they did in the past by speaking with the president of the condo corporation board or council to obtain their candid comments? Are there any complaints against them with the Better Business Bureau?

Have a lawyer check all the documents including the disclosure statement thoroughly before you ever make a purchase decision. Is there a time period within which you can get out of the deal and get your deposit money back? Make sure you pay your deposit only into a lawyer's trust account—your lawyer or the developer's lawyer. If there is a realtor involved, it could go into the realtors' trust account. In all cases, you want interest to be credited to you up till the day of completion. If you are buying into a phased development, you want to review all the documents to see what is intended to occur and when and where. You want to know, in writing, what the restrictions are on the total number of rental units permitted in the complex. Be cautious about construction warranties by the developer. They are only as strong as the developer. Many developers incorporate a new company for each development so that each risk is self-contained.

Some of the **advantages** of buying a new condo include:

- Flexibility in types of units available.
- Ability to upgrade features at the outset with customized change options.
- Ability to change the interior decorating to suit personal needs and wants.
- Built by current building code standards, which could be of higher quality.
- New Home Warranty coverage for financial protection.

Some of the **disadvantages** include:

- Your deposit funds will be held up until completion. However, if you make sure that you are getting interest on those funds to your credit, that reduces the discomfort.
- Construction delays are common for a variety of reasons. This could be inconvenient for you, especially if you are selling your present home and are relying on moving on the proposed completion date of the condo. You can try to negotiate a penalty clause into the offer agreement to buffer the risk, with X amount of money deducted from

the purchase price for each week of delay in completion. However, depending on circumstances and the developer, they may or may not go for it. Seek the advice of a lawyer to assist you in this area.

- If construction is not completed in other parts of the condo complex, other than your building, there could be noise and disruptive inconvenience for a period of time.

- As the project is conceptual in nature, rather than tangible, you will have to rely on artist renderings and floor plans. You will not be able to assess the quality of construction until the building is completed.

Buying a Presale Condo

In order for developers to test the market and obtain lender financing, they need to go through the stages of attempting to presale the condo units before construction can start. This process is normally done by having a sales office on the site of the future condo building, with artist renderings, architectural plans, scale models of the proposed development, etc. There would also probably be a sample showroom set up, showing the typical condo layout, types of furnishings to be supplied, such as carpets, cabinets, appliances, paint, fireplace, etc. The purpose is to try to simulate, as much as possible, what the final look and feel will be.

Many people like the idea of locking in a condo at the current price, paying a 5% or 10% down payment but not having to pay the full amount until the project is completed, which could be one to three years later. The length of time will depend on the nature of the project, the size of the developer, and availability of construction trades. Also, the lender generally wants to see at least 75% or more in presales before funding will be approved. A buyer of a presale condo in an escalating market could hope to obtain an attractive increase in equity before the project is even completed.

If you are seriously interested in buying a presale condo, you want to make sure that you read all the documents carefully and understand them and have a real estate lawyer advise you before you sign any contract or pay any down payment. You want to know the fine print, e.g., Can you get out of the deal with or without getting your deposit back and without any further legal commitment or liability? Can the developer adjust the price upward before closing due to market demand? You want to ensure that the funds are kept in a lawyer's trust account and that interest will accrue to your credit. You also want to know if there is a period of time in a presale condo situation where you can back out of the deal and get all your deposit money back—within 30 days, for example.

The same general cautions as outlined for new condos also apply to presale condos.

Tip #50: Know Your Warranty Coverage for a New Condo

If you are buying a new condo, it is very important that you investigate whether you are covered by new home warranty before you buy. This coverage will provide peace of mind and protect your financial investment. The coverage can vary between provinces and the plan involved.

Read the material and make sure you understand exactly what you are being covered for and what is not covered. If you have any questions, make sure you speak to a real estate lawyer before you financially commit yourself. This topic is discussed in detail in chapter 5. Also, refer to the Appendix under Helpful Websites for websites of companies that provide home warranty protection in your province.

Tip #51: How Do You Know If the Price Is Fair?

One of the most important steps you must take is to determine the worth of the property you are considering. In other words, how much should you pay for it? In theory, a property is worth whatever a buyer is prepared to pay for it and whatever the vendor is prepared to sell it for. There are various appraisal techniques that you can use, and that are used by professionally qualified appraisers. In addition, there are rules of thumb that real estate investors often use with revenue property. These rules of thumb are guidelines only. There are limitations to some of them in terms of their accuracy or acceptance.

Appraising the value of a property is more an art than a science. Two pieces of property are seldom identical. When a professional appraiser writes up a report, the estimate of value is given as an opinion, not a scientific fact. This is helpful to you as a basis for negotiation with the owner. The reliability of the appraisal, though, is directly related to the level of competence, integrity, experience, and objectivity of the appraiser, and the accuracy of information obtained. Real estate appraisal is only as reliable as the assumptions that are made. There are distinct benefits of having an appraisal, especially a professional appraisal.

Reasons for Obtaining an Appraisal

The main reasons you might want an appraisal would be to determine the following:

- A reasonable offering price for purchase purposes.

- Allocation of the purchase price to the land and building (revenue property).

- The value of a property for financing purposes (your lender will require this).

- The value of a property at death for estate purposes.

- The value of a property when converting the use from principal residence to investment (rental) use, or vice versa. This would be for Canada Revenue Agency capital gains determination purposes, unless you are exempt from this provision. Check with your accountant for more details.

- A reasonable asking price for sale purposes.

- The amount of insurance to carry.

- Undertaking a feasibility study of a purchase.

- Preparation for a property assessment appeal.

- Preparation for litigation purposes.

- To resolve a pricing dispute between joint owners of a property; or,

- To resolve a pricing dispute between business owners under a buy-sell agreement, or shareholders agreement, where the business owns a property.

- Preparation for a marital separation agreement or divorce.

- Preparation for expropriation negotiations.

- Preparation for taxation records or appeal purposes.

There are several professional designations for property appraisers in Canada. They subscribe to uniform academic, professional, and ethical standards, and are regulated by their professional associations. The most common national designations are AACI (Accredited Appraiser Canadian Institute) and CRA (Canadian Residential Appraiser), both awarded by the Appraisal Institute of Canada. There are some provincial appraisal designations, as well as specialty appraisal areas (e.g., industrial and commercial). Refer to the Helpful Websites section in the back of this book for contact information.

Determining the Value of a Condo

Here are some of the basic methods or rules of thumb used by professional appraisers, real estate lenders, or home buyers to determine the fair market value of a condo. If you are buying a condominium as a principal residence, you would normally only be interested in the **market comparison approach** and **cost approach**. The average of these two estimates is what most lenders use for value appraisal purposes. The lender then gives mortgage funds based on the purchase price or appraised value—whichever is lower. The purchaser pays for the appraisal cost (usually between $150 and $300) for the average house or condo purchase. The lender arranges for the appraisal.

If you intend to invest in real estate, there are many additional formulas to apply to determine value of revenue property. That is outside the scope of this book. If you are interested in investment real estate and evaluation criteria, refer to the latest edition of my book *Making Money in Real Estate: The Canadian Guide to Profitable Investment in Residential Property*. Also check out www.homebuyer.ca.

Market Comparison Approach

In effect, this approach is comparison shopping. It involves a comparison of similar properties to the one you are considering. Because no two properties are exactly the same due to age, location, layout, size, and features, etc., you want to attempt to obtain comparables as closely as possible. You want to have the sale dates as current as possible so that the comparison reflects the same market conditions.

You may have to make adjustments to the comparable properties to make the comparisons more realistic in determining prices; for example, making price adjustments in the comparison properties for such matters as the circumstances of the sale (e.g., forced sale due to financial problems, order for sale, foreclosure, etc.), special features of the property (e.g., flower garden, shrubs, arboretum, etc.), and location of property (view, privacy, etc.).

The market comparison approach lends itself to situations where the properties are more numerous and there are more frequent sales, and therefore they are easier to compare. Condominiums, single-family houses, and raw land are the most common types of properties to use the market comparison method. At least it gives you a feeling for the appropriate value.

Generally speaking, when an appraiser is doing a market comparison appraisal, he or she compares recent sales of similar properties, similar properties currently "listed" for sale on the market, and properties that did not sell, e.g., the listing has expired. The limitation of the market comparison approach is that similar properties may not be available for comparison in a particular situation. Also, it is difficult to know the motivations of the vendors of the comparable properties, so in some cases the sale price might not reflect the fair market value.

For example, if you are comparing a condominium for sale against two other identical condos in the same complex that have been sold very recently, that will give you a fairly close comparison. You could calculate the cost per square foot of the two recent condo sales and compare with the cost per square foot of the one you are considering. If that latter price is higher, you want to know why. Perhaps it has a better view, is on a higher floor, or the previous owner made a lot of interior decorating changes to improve the condo. The point is that the market comparison approach does have its limitations and provides general guidelines only.

Cost Approach

This approach involves calculating the cost to buy the land and to construct an equivalent type of building on the property you are considering with appropriate adjustments, and then comparing the end prices. There are various steps involved in arriving at a figure using the cost approach. It is an easier formula when buying a single-family house than a condominium. Because you would not likely be able to personally perform this calculation—it would normally be done by a professional appraiser—the discussion below is for your awareness only.

Step 1

Estimate the land value, using the market comparison approach discussed earlier. The sale price of similar vacant residential lots in the area should be determined, with adjustments made for such factors as use (zoning), size, location, and features (e.g., view).

Step 2

Estimate the cost to construct a new building that is comparable in square footage, features, and quality to the one that you are considering. For example, a modest-quality construction could be $50 per square foot to replace, whereas a luxury-quality construction could be $350 or more per square foot to replace.

Step 3

If the condo building you are considering is not new, you would have to calculate a depreciation factor (e.g., reduced value of the building because it is wearing out over time). Calculating the depreciation adjustment factor depends on the building's condition, age, and estimated useful life. Estimated useful life means the point beyond which the building is not economical to repair or maintain. In effect, it would have no market value. If that is the case, you might be buying primarily for lot value and intend to tear down the building or substantially renovate it. A professional appraiser would normally be required to calculate this depreciation factor.

Step 4

To determine estimated property value, add the depreciated cost of the building (Steps 2–3) to the cost of the land (Step 1).

For single-family houses and condominiums, the appraiser usually arrives at an estimate of value as of a certain date by adding the market and cost approach values, and dividing by two.

The limitation of the cost approach is that depreciation might be difficult to estimate correctly. In addition, construction costs vary, depending on location, supply and demand, and inflation. Again, the cost approach value is an estimate only.

This section has covered the two most common types of techniques for establishing the value of a property purchase for a principal-residence property. There are many other formulas that experienced or sophisticated investors may use in addition to the ones noted. The important point is to understand the basic concepts and to know when to apply them, to know their limitations, and to use several different formulas to provide some balance when comparing other properties as well as the property itself.

The key benefit of these methods is that they can often be quickly calculated to determine if the owner is asking too much, in terms of your purchase criteria, or if the sale is a bargain price. Remember, the rules of thumb are guidelines only. The calculations could also provide you with negotiating leverage to have the purchase price reduced. You will, of course, want to consider other factors before making your final decision. Also keep in mind that the values are estimates of what that average person would pay. You might decide to pay more, or offer less, in certain circumstances.

Tip #52: Factors that Drive Your Buying Position

You may not be prepared to pay the asking price for various reasons, including the following:

- The price is more than you can afford.
- The price is higher than your comfort level in terms of risk.
- The market is starting to decline.
- An economic downturn has begun.
- You aren't pressed to make a decision and can wait for a more attractive property.

Conversely, you might be prepared to pay more than the asking price. Here are some of the factors that might cause you to consider paying more:

Confidential Information

You might be aware of a possible zoning change, subdivision potential, or proposed development nearby.

Financing

You might be able to obtain favourable financial terms (e.g., a low-interest vendor-back mortgage or high-ratio financing).

Potential for High Income

The property could have a revenue-generating suite.

Attractive Closing Date

You could get a long closing date, enabling you to get funds that you are expecting from various sources, or to obtain access to higher mortgage financing by closing, or to sell the agreement of purchase and sale to someone else (almost like having an option).

Personal Income Tax Bracket

Depending on your personal situation, you may be able to offset a negative cash flow against your other income and thus buy a revenue property at a discount price because of the negative cash flow. You would be relying on appreciation and a capital gain, or know how to change the negative cash flow to positive over time.

Required Return on Your Investment

You might have a lower requirement for your return on this investment than others, if you are buying a revenue property.

Tip #53: How to Prepare for Negotiation

Understanding the art of negotiation is going to be important for you if you want to make your best deal—both as a buyer and seller. Whether you are a first-time home buyer, or an experienced or novice real estate investor, you will benefit from the practical tips and street-smart strategies and insights presented below.

Most interaction with people—professionals, business associates, suppliers—involves some dynamics of the negotiation process. If you are attempting to sell, persuade, convince, or influence another person's thinking or feeling to accord with your own wants and needs, you are using negotiating skills. If, at the same time, you have defined and satisfied the other person's needs, you have attained an optimal or "win-win" type of negotiation. However, in practical terms in real estate negotiations, you may not satisfy the seller's or buyer's needs, as their needs and expectations may be unrealistic in the circumstances.

There are psychological negotiating games and techniques abundantly used in the real estate market by different players. They will help you save more money and therefore make more money on any type of real estate purchase or sale.

This tip will discuss the necessary steps to follow to prepare for real estate negotiation, understanding the reasons why the property might be for sale, and what to put in the offer.

Be Prepared

There are preliminary steps you should take to maximize your success before any offer is made:

- Determine the amount of mortgage that you are entitled to, the maximum price that you are prepared to pay, and the terms that you would prefer.
- Have alternative properties in mind so that you have fallbacks.
- Have your realtor thoroughly check out the property. Find out such factors as how long it has been for sale, why it is for sale, how the vendor determined the asking price, recent market comparables in the area, and any vendor deadline pressure.
- Ideally, use a realtor as a negotiating buffer between you and the vendor.
- Obtain legal and tax advice on the implications of your purchase.
- Don't get emotionally involved with the property. Be totally objective and realistic; otherwise, it could taint your judgment.
- Train yourself to appear patient and objective to the vendor or vendor's agent. Don't show your emotions, but be businesslike.

- To increase your bargaining leverage, look for negative features of the property in advance. All properties can be found to have some kind of drawback. For example, property taxes could be very high, or the building might be showing signs of age or disrepair. Write down a list of the positive and negative features.

- Arrange to have the services of a home inspector available on short notice.

Tip #54: The Fine Print of Presenting an Offer

Following are some guidelines when presenting an offer:

Name of Purchaser

Depending on the nature of your purchase, you may want to put your name and the words "or assignee" if it is your intent to sign over the agreement to someone else. However, it is legally questionable whether such a designation would be enforceable if a dispute arose. Alternatively, if you are purchasing an investment or speculative property with a degree of risk, you may want to incorporate a company and put the offer in the corporate name. If you back out of the deal before closing, your company could be sued for breach of contract and damages (losses) by the vendor, but not you personally. Presumably your new company will not have any assets at that stage. You need experienced legal advice in advance if you are considering any of the above scenarios, due to the potential risk.

Deposit

Try to put the smallest deposit down. You don't want to tie up any more money than you have to. Also, if you back out prior to closing, your deposit funds could be at risk of being kept by the vendor. Whatever deposit money you put down, never pay it directly to the vendor. Always have it paid to a realtor's or lawyer's trust account. Make sure you write in the offer that your deposit funds are to accrue interest to your credit pending the closing date.

Price

Attempt to offer the lowest possible price the market and circumstances allow. Always start with your ideal price and terms. You never know what the vendor will find to be acceptable or not, so don't anticipate an unfavourable reaction. Think positively. If the vendor counter-offers, think of it as an opportunity to move the deal forward.

Closing Date

Depending on your objectives, you may want to have a long closing date such as three or four months. Perhaps you will be in receipt of funds by then if you are selling your present home. Personal reasons also enter into the time frame of the closing date.

Financing Terms

You may want to ask the vendor for vendor-back financing for a first or second mortgage. Depending on your objectives, you may want to ask for a long-term open mortgage (say, five years) with an attractive interest rate, and assumable without qualifications. This latter provision would make it easier for resale. The vendor may be willing to provide such favourable terms if the market is slow and he is anxious to sell.

Conditions

Conditions are sometimes referred to as "subject" clauses. You should include as many conditional clauses as you feel are appropriate for your needs, such as subject to "financing" or "building inspection satisfactory to the purchaser." Also include any warranty confirmations from the vendor. (Conditions are covered in detail in chapter 5.)

Tip #55: Get Title Insurance

Many lenders and borrowers are now taking out title insurance. This type of insurance protects you in case there are any defects in the title of the property;

or charges or claims that have not been filed on the property title; or were filed, but not picked up on the searches before ownership passed to you. For example, maybe a survey was not done, or it was an old property survey, and the boundaries of your property are not what you thought you were getting. Title insurance could also cover you for mortgages that were discharged and paid out but still remain on title, and certain construction liens.

Another benefit of title insurance is to protect you from title fraud. Here are some examples:

- Someone fraudulently refinances your property by forging your signature and using fake identification, then obtains the funds and cannot be found. You are left to defend your title and pay all the legal costs.

- Someone fraudulently transfers the title of your property out of your name by forging your signature and using fake identification. They then obtain a mortgage, or several mortgages, on the property without your knowledge and cannot be found. You are left with the responsibility of paying the mortgage and reclaiming your property ownership.

You can imagine the prolonged stress, uncertainty, negative energy, time, and legal costs of trying to protect your property rights and dealing with the financial fraud. If you had the right type of title insurance, you would have peace of mind. The insurance covers you from the time you take title until you sell your home. Title insurance will cover you for your legal fees to defend your right of ownership, which could cost tens of thousands of dollars, as well as your actual financial losses. You can see why so many Canadian homeowners want to have the protection of title insurance. For more information, refer to the Appendix under Helpful Websites.

Tip #56: Typical Costs When Closing a Purchase

Here are the typical costs that may or may not be applicable in your circumstances. Discuss these costs with your lawyer and be aware of the money you'll need at closing.

- Deposit
- Mortgage application fee

- Property appraisal
- Property inspection
- Balance of purchase price
- Legal fees re: property transfer
- Legal fees re: mortgage preparation
- Legal disbursements re: property transfer
- Legal disbursements re: mortgage preparation
- Mortgage broker commission
- Property survey
- Property tax holdback (by mortgage company)
- Land transfer or deed tax (provincial)
- Property purchase tax (provincial)
- Property tax adjustment (local/municipal)
- Goods and Services Tax (federal)
- New Home Warranty Program fee
- Mortgage interest adjustment (by mortgage company)
- Provincial sales tax on chattels purchased from vendor
- Adjustments for fuel, taxes, etc.
- Mortgage lender insurance premium (CMHC or Genworth Financial)
- Condominium maintenance fee adjustment
- Home and property insurance
- Life insurance premium on amount of outstanding mortgage
- Moving expenses
- Utility connection charges
- Home and garden implements
- Redecorating and refurbishing costs
- Immediate repair and maintenance costs

Tip #57: You Can't Hide from the Taxman

Tax is a particularly important consideration, whether you are buying a condominium as a principal residence or investment property. The information and tips below will save you money, or at least help you to understand the key options open to you to save money. As income tax provisions can change at any time, before making any real estate purchase plans for investment purposes, make sure you contact a tax accountant to obtain current income tax advice. Everyone's tax situation is unique to his or her own personal circumstances.

The following discussion highlights the main categories of local, provincial, and federal government taxes when dealing with a home used as a principal residence. Note that if you have a second property or other revenue property, there are different tax considerations.

Local/Municipal Taxes

Municipalities assess taxes for various purposes. Some municipalities include all taxes within one assessment. Others separate the taxes out. The main taxes are as follows. (To obtain further information about local taxes, contact city hall or your lawyer.)

Property Taxes

These are generally due on an annual basis with assessment of value determined within six months prior to the property taxation year. For residential property, a "mill rate" is generally determined annually and multiplied by the assessed value of the property, including the building on the property, to determine the actual tax due. In many provinces, there is a homeowner's grant that is subtracted from the gross taxes assessed for your property to determine the net payable tax you owe. As you might assume, this annual grant is for a principal residence only, and not an investment property. The grant amount can vary depending on the age of the homeowner.

If you believe your property taxes are unfair because they are based on an artificially high property assessment of value, you can appeal the assessment notice. For example, when a real estate market has gone down, it is not uncommon for property assessment appeals to increase because of the time it takes for the assessment to reflect the reduction in value.

Property taxes are generally assessed for services supplied by the municipality such as schools, education, roads, hospitals, etc.

Utility Taxes

These taxes tend to be for such services as water, sewer, garbage pick-up, etc.

Provincial Taxes

Many provincial governments charge a property purchase tax when purchasing a property. This is the main form of provincial tax dealing with property. To obtain more information about provincial taxes, contact your provincial government, lawyer or local branch of your provincial government land titles office.

Property Purchase Tax

Essentially, this tax is assessed at the time of purchase and a fee is charged based on the purchase price of the property. It is paid at the time of purchase. The formula for determining the amount payable varies between provinces.

Federal Taxes

There are two main federal taxes: the Goods & Services Tax (GST) and income tax.

Here is an overview. To obtain more information on the GST or income tax, contact the Canada Revenue Agency (CRA) or your accountant. All government listings are located in the Blue Pages of your phone book. (Also refer to the Appendix under Helpful Websites for the CRA's website.)

Goods and Services Tax (GST)

The GST applies to every "supply" of real property, both residential and commercial, unless the "supply" can fit within one of the exemptions set out in the legislation.

The term *supply* has broad meaning. It includes not only sales and leases of real property but also transfers, exchanges, barters, and gifts. Most services dealing with real estate transaction are also covered by the GST. In other words, whenever you consume a "good" (i.e., buy a product or use a service), you will be required, in most cases, to pay the 7% tax.

The following overview discusses how certain types of real estate purchases are affected by or exempted from the GST, and how the GST rebate system operates. As government policies and criteria change from time to time, check with your real estate lawyer or accountant for a current update.

How the GST System Works

The GST is paid by the purchaser to the vendor at the time of purchase. The vendor then remits the tax to the CRA. Sometimes the vendor includes the GST within the purchase price and other times it may be added on separately. There are also several categories of GST exemptions relating to real estate.

If you are the purchaser having to pay the GST, you may be able to receive a partial rebate or offset GST tax paid against GST tax received. It depends on whether you purchased the property as a principal residence, for investment purposes, or are in the business of buying and selling properties.

The GST and Resale Condominiums

If you buy a used residential property as a principal residence, there is no GST payable on the purchase price. In other words, it is exempt. CRA defines "used residential property" to include an owner-occupied house, condominium, duplex, apartment building, vacation property, summer cottage, or non-commercial hobby farm. The "used" property definition requires that the vendor must not be a "builder" as defined in the legislation. A builder is someone who builds or substantially renovates the property as a business. Used property can also mean a recently built house that is substantially complete and has been sold at least once before you buy it.

If you purchase a resale home that includes a room used as an office, and you are self-employed, the entire house still qualifies for the GST exemption if you use it primarily as your residence. However, if you purchase a home that is used primarily for commercial business purposes, and it is zoned for that type of operation, at the time of purchase you would only be GST exempt from the portion that you will reside in.

When purchasing a resale home, you can request that the vendor provide you with a certificate stating that the property qualifies as "used" for GST purposes.

The GST and New Condominiums

When you purchase a newly constructed home from a builder as a principal residence for yourself or a relative, the entire purchase price, including the land, is taxable. The word *home* refers to a residential dwelling and includes a single-family house, condominium (apartment or townhouse format), or mobile home. If the home is going to be your principal residence, it may qualify for a partial GST rebate, depending upon the sale price.

Purchasers of homes priced up to $350,000 will qualify for the maximum rebate of $8,750, or 36% of the GST paid on the purchase price, whichever is less. Since the $8,750 amount is 2.5% of $350,000, a purchaser is really paying the GST at a rate of 4.5% on a $350,000 home, instead of 7%.

If you are purchasing a home priced at more than $350,000 but less than $450,000, the rebate is gradually reduced, in other words, declines to zero on a proportional basis. There is no rebate for homes selling for $450,000 or more.

If you are purchasing the home for investment purposes and you intend to rent out the property to tenants, the full 7% GST is charged on the purchase price and no rebate is available. If you are purchasing the home through a limited company, a rebate is not allowed.

Here are some examples of how the rebate is calculated if you are buying for a principal residence. The term *purchase price* refers to the price paid to the builder for the home and lot before the GST is calculated, and does not include any associated realty or legal fees.

The GST and Real Estate Transaction Expenses

Most of the services associated with completing a real estate transaction are eligible to have the GST applied. For example, the GST is applied to the commission that a real estate agent charges for facilitating a sale. The tax is paid by the person responsible for paying the commission, usually the vendor. Real estate commissions are GST taxable, even if the total GST owed is reduced by a rebate or the sale is exempt from the GST. For example, if you sell a used home, the sale price is exempt from the GST, but the real estate commission is still taxable.

Other real estate–related services on which the GST is charged include fees for surveys, inspections, appraisals, and legal and tax advice. The GST is charged on these fees regardless of whether the house you purchase is exempt from the tax. All moving charges are taxed.

There are several exemptions from the GST, however. Mortgage broker fees are not taxed if the fees are charged separately from any taxable real estate commissions. Also, a mortgage and the interest on mortgages are exempt from the GST.

GST and Condominium Maintenance Fees

If you own a condominium, the monthly fee charged by the condominium corporation is not subject to the GST. However, the condominium corporation will be charged GST on all services employed to maintain the building and grounds. These additional GST costs will obviously be passed on to the condominium owners in the form of increased monthly fees.

GST and Homeowner Expenses

Any service you employ around the house, such as gardening, plumbing, carpentry, etc., will carry a 7% charge. You will already know there is a GST charge on your cable, hydro, and telephone bills.

Tip #58: Income Tax and Your Personal Residence

There are many tax considerations you should be aware of when buying real estate for personal use or for investment purposes. Here are some highlights.

For most people, their first investment in real estate is their first home that they will occupy. Your principal residence may be a house, apartment, condominium, duplex, mobile home, or a houseboat. A property will generally qualify as a principal residence if it meets various conditions:

- You must own the property solely or jointly with another person.

- You, your spouse, your former spouse or one of your children ordinarily inhabited it at some point during the year.
- You consider the property your principal residence.

One of the key benefits is that the gain you realize on the sale of the home that was your principal residence is not subject to capital gains tax. For example, if you buy a condo for $100,000 and sell it for $175,000, you would not pay tax on the gain, which is $75,000.

Tip #59: Capital Gains or Income on an Investment Property?

Many investors assume that when property is sold for a profit, the profit will be treated as a capital gain for income tax purposes. This would result in a lower tax rate than other types of income. You have to be very careful, though, as CRA could consider the profit as regular income at regular tax rates.

Capital gains are usually taxed at 50% of the capital gain. In other words, if you bought a property for $100,000 and sold it for $225,000, but after all expenses were taken into account you net $200,000, the net profit (gain) would be approximately $100,000. You would normally have to pay tax on 50% of the net gain, or $50,000. If the profit were deemed to be income instead of a capital gain, you would have to pay tax on 100% of the amount—the full $100,000.

CRA applies various types of criteria to determine if the profit is deemed to be a capital gain from a real estate investment, or income from a business of speculating in real estate without any investment intent. Each situation depends on the individual circumstances, so make sure you get tax advice from a professional accountant in advance.

For example, if you purchased a property with the intention of selling it as soon as possible, e.g., in a "hot" real estate market, that could be deemed to be income. In other words, you "flipped" the property or sold your rights under an agreement of purchase and sale. Another example would be in a situation where a person bought vacant land with the intention of selling it quickly. The key tests are what your original intent was when you purchased the property, the facts and the circumstances, and how quickly you sold it. There are many credible and logical reasons to refute the income theory and argue that it should be considered a capital gain. It would be very frustrating to plan on specific after-tax money from a sale, and then find that you owe more money to CRA than you had planned. That is why you need good tax planning and advice from a professional accountant, a point that is reinforced throughout this book.

Tip #60: Income Tax and Investment Property

If you decide to invest in a condominium rental property, many of your personal expenses may be deducted from income in addition to the normal tax deductions such as mortgage, interest, depreciation, and other condominium-related expenses. For example, you would normally be entitled to set up a small office in your current residence for managing your investments, which would include keeping your records. You could deduct a percentage of all your home-related expenses. The normal formula is to take the square footage of the office area that you are using relative to the total square footage in your home. In general terms, 10% to 15% or more is usually deductible for that portion.

In addition, you would be entitled to deduct a part of the car-related expenses involved in managing your investment portfolio, whether it is one rental property or more than one. The percentage of all your car-related expenses can vary, obviously depending on the usage of the car relating to your investment.

It is essential that you obtain advice from a professional tax accountant familiar with real estate issues before you make a decision about buying a condo as a real estate investment. Laws and regulations dealing with taxation matters are complex and constantly changing. Also, you will want to have specific advice based on your personal circumstances. In addition, there are forms, guides, information criteria, and interpretation bulletins available from CRA. Make sure you obtain the Rental Income Guide for further tax details. Look in the Blue Pages of your telephone directory under "Government of Canada." (Refer to the Appendix under Helpful Websites for the CRA website.)

Tip #61: Can You Have a Rental Suite in Your Condo?

It is not uncommon for people to want to rent out part of their principal residence as an income source or "mortgage helper." This is not practical in apartment-type condos, but could be in townhouse condos or bare land condos in detached homes. Whether the condominium corporation permits renting out part of your condo depends on the bylaws, and rules and regulations. You need to check that out thoroughly first, and get consent in writing. If you pass that acid test, the next issue is municipal bylaws about "secondary suites," which are sometimes referred to as "illegal suites." This term refers to the fact that the suite or room rented to someone who is not a relative may contravene existing municipal zoning bylaws in the community in which you reside. The zoning for your home might be "single family" and renting part of your home to a tenant, in effect, means you are arbitrarily converting your home into a multi-family dwelling.

The federal government does not care whether your rental space contravenes municipal zoning bylaws or not. All CRA cares about is whether or not you are reporting the income in your tax returns.

In practical terms, many municipalities do not enforce the bylaw regulations relating to "illegal suites" if there is a shortage of rental accommodation in the community, or unless a neighbour complains. In most cases you have a right to appeal a decision of your municipality requesting that the tenant vacate your premises. Each situation can vary. If in doubt, contact your lawyer for advice.

Understanding Capital Cost Allowance (CCA) and Expenses

If you are renting out one or two rooms of your home to a boarder, it will not interfere with its principal residence status as long as you do not claim capital cost allowance (CCA) on the rental portion. Essentially, CCA means depreciating a portion of the value of the home, excluding land, and deducting that portion as an expense from your income. In addition, the rental portion is supposed to be minor in relation to the whole house, e.g., 10% to 25%, although in some cases this can be up to 50% or more. For peace of mind, speak to your tax accountant.

If you do rent out part of your principal residence, you can deduct many types of expenses from your income. The net effect might be that your expenses (excluding CCA, of course), exceed or equal the income, meaning that you have no tax payable to CRA.

The normal expenses would be for things such as interest on your mortgage, property taxes, maintenance and repairs, insurance premiums, light, heat, and water, and advertising. Expenses specifically related to the rented part of the building may be claimed in full. However, expenses that relate to the whole property must be apportioned between rental and personal use. You may base the apportionment on square feet/metres or the number of rooms rented in the condo, as long as it is done on a reasonable basis.

You are supposed to fill out a "Statement of Real Estate Rentals" and include it with your personal income tax. This form, along with examples, is inside the Rental Income Tax Guide that you can obtain from CRA.

Tip #62: Operating a Home Business from Your Condo

Many people, at some point, intend to start a part-time or full-time business out of their home. There is a growing trend in this area for various reasons, including eliminating daily commuting to work, lifestyle choice (e.g., to raise a family), retirement opportunity, supplementing salaried income, testing a business idea, or saving on business overhead and thereby reducing financial risk by writing off home-related expenses. There are many different types of home-based service businesses that lend themselves to operating out of a condo. For example: consulting, counseling, computer-based business, telephone sales, tutoring, teaching small groups, research, travel agent, etc. In other words, you would not have people coming to your home in great numbers, if at all, so you would be operating below the radar screen of nuisance to your neighbours.

For more detail on starting up a home business or small business, refer to the latest edition of my book *The Complete Canadian Small Business Guide* or check out the website www.smallbiz.ca. It is important to keep in mind that you need competent tax and legal advice before you start up. This book contains general guidelines only.

Getting a GST Number

You must obtain a GST number if you have over $30,000 in income in your business, or are paying GST on items you purchase and want to set off against GST you are charging. Check with your accountant and closest GST office.

Canada Revenue Agency allows you to have a business at home without affecting the principal residence status, as long as you don't claim CCA on your home as part of your business operation. You can claim CCA on other non-home business capital expenditures, according to the CCA class. Again, speak to your accountant.

Claiming Expenses

There are numerous categories of expenses that can be deducted depending on the nature of your business. An expense is deductible if its purpose is to earn income, it is not of a capital nature (e.g., depreciated over time by using CCA), and is reasonable in the circumstances. Your professional accountant will advise you as to which expenses are deductible and which are not. The suggestions or examples outlined in this tip are only guidelines. Also, if some of the expenses are related to personal use, you are required to deduct that portion from the business expense. Reasonable salaries paid to a spouse and/or children for services rendered to the business are also deductible. The "Statement of Income and Expenses" form from CRA outlines some of the expenses that you may wish to consider. This form is contained in the Business and Professional Income Tax Guide. Your accountant may suggest other expenses that you could be eligible for. Check out the CRA website and www.smallbiz.ca.

Also, the expenses you may deduct for the business use of your home cannot exceed the income from the business for which you use the workspace. This means that you must not use these expenses to create or increase your business loss. You may carry forward any expenses that are not deductible in the year and deduct them, subject to the same limitation, in the following year.

To deduct expenses, you take that portion relating to the space used for home office use. For example, you can divide the total number of rooms in the house by the number of rooms used for business, to find the percentage of square feet used for business. So if you were using 20% of your home for business purposes, including the basement for storage of inventory (e.g., if you have a townhouse type of condo or bare land condo with a detached dwelling), then you would deduct 20% of all your related expenses from your business income.

There are direct and indirect expenses relating to your home business that are deductible in part or in full. Here is a description of the most common expenses that apply to your condo unit. There are more expenses such as travel, entertainment, and auto, which are not discussed here but which can be discussed with your accountant. As a reminder, be aware of the fact that tax law changes can and do occur from time to time, which could affect any of the following deductions.

Maximizing Expense Deductions

Direct Business Expenses

These are expenses that would only benefit the business part of the home. Some of these costs are depreciated (applying CCA) and others are deducted:

- Room Furnishings

  Office furniture and equipment would have to be depreciated (use the CCA schedule obtained from CRA or your accountant). Other items such as office supplies and materials can be deducted.

- Remodelling or Decorating Costs

  This would include repairs or renovations done to a room to turn it into an office (e.g., painting, carpentry, floor covering, plumbing, electrical, etc.). If you added an extension to your house, that would be covered as well. This should be listed as an improvement and should be depreciated as discussed under "room furnishings" above.

Combined Business/Personal Expenses

These are expenses that benefit both the personal and the business parts of the home business, but only the business part is deductible as a business expense. Expenses should be apportioned on a reasonable basis between business and non-business use (e.g., a percentage of the floor space used). These are only guidelines, so make sure you obtain customized professional tax advice from a qualified accountant.

Rent

If you live in your principal residence condo and use part of it for business purposes, you may deduct the portion of your rent attributable to business use. For example, you may decide to claim 20% of your unit as "rent." Common ranges for a condo would be from 10% to 25%. It could be more, of course, depending on use. Speak to your accountant.

Mortgage Interest

You can deduct the percentage of interest expense related to use of your home for business. For example, if your monthly mortgage payments are $2,000, generally about 99% of that payment is interest and 1% goes toward the principal. This would be the case, especially in the first three years of the mortgage (assuming it is a 25-year amortization period). Therefore, for practical purposes, let's assume the interest portion is $2,000. If you were claiming 20% of your house as business-use related, you would claim $400 per month, multiplied by 12 months, which would equal $4,800 a year as a business expense.

Insurance Premiums

You can deduct that portion of insurance expense that relates to your business (e.g., fire, theft, liability coverage). If you were claiming 20% usage of your house or apartment, you would claim that portion of the premium as a business expense.

Depreciation of Your Home

In practical terms, most home business owners do not claim CCA on their principal residence. The reason is that if you later dispose of the property, a taxable capital gain could arise on the portion of the property that you used for business purposes. You could also be subject to recapture (having to claim on the following year's tax return as income) of the CCA previously claimed. You don't want to taint the principal residence tax-free capital gains status. Speak to your accountant.

Utilities

You can deduct the portion of your expenses related to business (e.g., 20%) for gas, electrical, water costs, etc. You could deduct 100% of your cable charges if they are for business use, or a portion otherwise. Your Internet connection is 100% deducible if just for business use, or a portion otherwise.

Home Maintenance

You can deduct a portion of your expenses for labour and materials for house maintenance and repairs for business use (e.g., furnace or roof repair). You cannot claim, however, for your own labour. You may be able to pay other family members for labour, as long as it is reasonable, i.e., within the range that you would pay a third party to perform the services.

Services

You can deduct a portion of municipal or private services such as snow and trash removal, yard maintenance, etc., for business use.

Telephone

If you have a separate telephone and business line, the full amount of costs is deductible (e.g., monthly service charge). If you were using your residence phone for business use, you would deduct the portion of costs that is business-related. All long-distance charges that are business related are of course totally deductible. Other phone-related costs that you could deduct (in full or in part) would be installation costs, telephone equipment, answering machine or voice mail, or answering service.

Tip #63: What Are Typical Preparation Pitfalls to Avoid?

Being aware of the potential problems with condo ownership and investing should help you avoid common pitfalls, hassle, stress, and financial loss. This tip, and the next six, places the cautions of this book in context. Points under certain tips are repeated in some cases in other categories of tips, as they apply in both categories.

Here are some typical pitfalls to avoid when doing the initial preparation to buy a condo:

- Not having an understanding of how the real estate market works.
- Not buying real estate at the right time in the market.

- Not having a clear understanding of personal and financial wants and needs.

- Not having a clear focus and lacking a realistic purchase plan, with strategies and priorities.

- Not doing thorough market research and comparison shopping before making the purchase.

- Not selecting the right property considering the potential risks, money involved, and specific personal needs.

- Not seeing the property before buying it, but relying on pictures, the Internet, and/or the representations of others.

- Not buying for the right reasons. For example, buying for tax shelter inducement reasons, rather than the inherent value, potential, and viability of the investment property.

Tip #64: What Are Typical Due Diligence Pitfalls to Avoid?

When buying a condo, it is important to do your due diligence. This means being thorough in your research and review of documentation. You need to understand what documentation is important and why, and need to understand the implications of the documentation. Here are some pitfalls to avoid when doing your due diligence:

- Not verifying representations or assumptions beforehand.

- Not making a decision based on an objective assessment, but on an emotional one.

- Not determining the real reason why the vendor is selling.

- Not having the property inspected by a qualified home inspector before finalizing the purchase.

- Not selecting an experienced real estate lawyer and obtaining advice beforehand.

- Not selecting an experienced professional tax accountant when selecting real estate investment property, and obtaining tax and accounting advice beforehand.

- Not selecting an experienced realtor who has expertise in the type of real estate and geographic location you are considering.

- Not independently verifying financial information beforehand. For example, the condo financial statements, condo minutes of the previous two years, etc.

- Not obtaining and reviewing all the necessary documentation appropriate for the condo before making a final decision to buy. Some of the common documents that may or may not be applicable (terminology could vary among provinces) would be: project documents (disclosure/declaration) prospectus, financial statements, rules and regulations, bylaws, estoppel certificate, etc.

- Not having an independent third party review the key documents and provide candid feedback. For example, lawyer, accountant, obtaining a consultation from a competing property management company to review documents, etc.

- Not checking out the property. For example, speaking with neighbours, others in the condo development, checking out the builder's reputation if a new building or presale, speaking with the condo management company agent and president of the condo board or council.

- Not selecting real estate partners carefully, whether buying for investment or any other type of joint purchase.

Tip #65: What Are Typical Partnership Pitfalls to Avoid?

If you are buying a condo with someone else, you need to be cautious of the legal implications. This is the case whether you are in a married or common-law relationship, or buying with friends or family, or for investment purposes.

- Not understanding the legal implications of owning real estate in joint tenancy or tenancy-in-common.

- Not understanding the legal implications of a claim for property ownership in the event of a break-up in a common-law relationship.

- Not writing down your needs, wants, and expectations with respect to the real estate partnership relationship, so you can talk candidly about them with your real estate partners.

- Not understanding the implications of buying real estate with family or friends. For example, the need for legal documentation in advance setting out the expectations and terms of agreement, renovations, sharing of costs for maintenance and expenses, sale criteria and timing, pricing, etc. You want to avoid conflict at all costs, as you want the friendship to survive the joint real estate purchase. For example, you might be buying a recreational property for joint use. You need to set out in writing the nature of use to avoid any misunderstandings. For example: times of use by different families, repair and maintenance and sharing of costs, furniture and furnishings, criteria for sale or purchase by other partners, formulas for resolving disputes or disagreements, etc.

- Not selecting real estate investment partners carefully. You need to apply the SWOT test: Strengths, Weaknesses, Opportunities, and Threats. Here are the key factors to consider when buying real estate with others: goals and objectives, expertise, liquidity, liability, legal structure, control issues, tax considerations, compatibility, risk assessment, contribution, percentage of investment, getting out or getting others out, management, and profits and losses.

- Not understanding the legal implications of different formats of group investing in real estate, such as: co-tenancy, general partnership, limited partnership, corporation, joint venture, syndication, equity sharing, etc.

Tip #66: What Are Typical Financing Pitfalls to Avoid?

When arranging for financing, there are lots of pitfalls to avoid that could make the difference in how much you pay for your mortgage, how much you pay to get out of it if necessary, and whether you have other hassles. Here are some of the classic pitfalls:

- Not doing financial calculations and projections beforehand.

- Not buying at a fair market price.

- Not buying within financial debt-servicing capacity, comfort zone, and skills.

- Not having a financial budget for condo-related expenses once ownership occurs.
- Not budgeting for closing costs when ownership changes hands.
- Not understanding the financing game thoroughly, and therefore not comparison shopping and not getting the best rates, terms, and right type of mortgage.
- Not obtaining quotes from a minimum of three mortgage brokers.
- Not obtaining a pre-approved mortgage to have a realty and reality check.
- Not knowing the pros and cons of a variable rate mortgage over a fixed-term mortgage.
- Not getting a release of liability from your mortgage company before a buyer assumes your existing mortgage.
- Not getting experienced tax advice before buying property for investment.
- Not selling your existing property before committing to buy a new property, and therefore risking having to debt-service both properties.

Tip #67: What Are Typical Legal Pitfalls to Avoid?

All the documentation involved with buying a condo has legal implications, so there are lots of legal pitfalls to avoid. Here are some of the main ones:

- Not selecting an experienced real estate lawyer and obtaining advice before any documents are signed.
- Not reviewing and understanding all the condo legal documents beforehand. For example, bylaws and rules and regulations, financial statements, previous two years of condo minutes, etc.
- Not putting in the appropriate conditions or "subject clauses" in the offer.
- Not having a written agreement with real estate investment partners, prepared by a lawyer.
- Not precisely and exactly setting out what fixtures and chattels are included in the purchase price.

- Not verifying vendor representations or buyer assumptions before-hand.

- Not having home office supplemental insurance if operating a home office.

- Not having adequate or appropriate insurance coverage for the risk and nature of principal residence or investment property. For example, if renting out part of the principal residence to a tenant (such as a mortgage-helper suite in basement), you should have specific extra insurance protection. If renting out a second property periodically or seasonally, you should have specific coverage for that use, or a claim could be denied. Need to speak to a knowledgeable insurance broker.

- Not having a valid and current will based on legal and tax advice.

Tip #68: What Are Typical Investment Pitfalls to Avoid?

If you are thinking of investing in real estate, there are extra pitfalls and traps to avoid. Here are the most common ones, some of which have been repeated in the tips on owning real estate with partners:

- Not understanding the implications of buying real estate with family or friends. For example, the need for legal documentation in advance setting out the expectations and terms of agreement, renovations, sale criteria, pricing, problem resolution formulas, etc.

- Not selecting real estate investment partners carefully. You need to apply the SWOT test: Strengths, Weaknesses, Opportunities, and Threats. Here are the key factors to consider when buying real estate with others: goals and objectives, expertise, liquidity, liability, legal structure, control issues, tax considerations, compatibility, risk assessment, contribution, percentage of investment, getting out or getting others out, management, and profits and losses.

- Not understanding the legal implications of different formats of group investing in real estate, such as: co-tenancy, general partnership, limited partnership, corporation, joint venture, syndication, equity sharing, etc.

- Not using the professional services in advance of a real estate lawyer.

- Not using the professional services in advance of a qualified tax advisor and accountant.

- Not using the services of an experienced and knowledgeable realtor.

- Not having the personality or the time to be suited to being a landlord.

- Not using the services of a professional real estate management company when circumstances would suggest that option would be prudent.

- Not understanding the rights and obligations of landlords and tenants under provincial legislation.

- Not having a legally customized rental application form and rental agreement for tenants to sign that supplements provincial legislation. This form would deal with issues such as pets, smoking, parties, noise, number of occupants, etc.

- Not reading my comprehensive book on real estate investing in Canada! It is called *Making Money in Real Estate: The Canadian Guide to Profitable Investment in Residential Property*, 2nd edition, published by John Wiley & Sons.

- Not referring to the articles, checklists, and newsletter on my website! That is: www.homebuyer.ca. Also check out www.smallbiz.ca.

Tip #69: What Are Typical Tax Pitfalls to Avoid?

When buying real estate for your principal residence, or for investment purposes, you need to know the tax issues and strategies. Here are the typical tax pitfalls to avoid:

- Not getting tax advice in advance from an experienced and qualified tax accountant, such as a chartered accountant or certified general accountant.

- Not applying tax strategies when buying or selling a second recreational property. For example, determining the ownership of the property and whether in joint tenancy or tenancy-in-common, in order to maximize the tax savings on sale or transfer or death, and minimize or eliminate the capital gains tax hit.

- Not having a valid and current will developed after professional tax and legal advice to minimize or defer the tax impact on death, if property is in your name.

- Not considering the potential benefits of owning property in a corporation or by means of a trust.

- Not having an overall estate plan to integrate strategies for all your assets and investments. Refer to my book (co-authored with John Budd) *The Canadian Guide to Will and Estate Planning*, 2nd edition, published by McGraw-Hill Ryerson. Check out www.estateplanning.ca.

Tip #70: What Are Typical Selling Pitfalls to Avoid?

When you buy real estate, you want to maximize the financial benefit on sale whether it is your principal residence or investment property. Here are some of the common pitfalls to avoid when selling a property:

- Not having a strategic plan when selling your property.

- Not selling the property at the right time or the right (realistic) price.

- Not using the services of a realtor but selling the property yourself. Although one can be a FISBO (for sale by owner) there are risks and limitations that you need to consider, which have been covered in this book.

- Not comparison shopping to select an experienced realtor knowledgeable of your geographic area.

- Not requiring the realtor to give you a written plan in advance, detailing the specifics of the marketing that will be done for your property.

- Not looking at your property objectively but emotionally.

- Not considering the tax implications (such as capital gains tax) of the timing or format of your sale if an investment property.

- Not giving your home curb-appeal by updating and maintaining the home and grounds.

CHAPTER 5

Legal Aspects of Buying a Condo

There are many legal considerations involved in buying a condo. You need to have an awareness of the key issues so that you can discuss them with your lawyer in an informed fashion. This will enhance the quality of your decision-making and minimize your financial, legal, and insurance risks.

Tip #71: Know the Difference Between Freehold and Leasehold Interest in Land

There are several types of legal interests in land, the most common being freehold and leasehold.

Freehold Interest

This type of ownership in land entitles the owner to use the land for an indefinite period of time and to deal with the land in any way he wishes, subject to legislation (for example, the Condominium Act), contractual obligations (e.g., declaration, rules and regulations, etc.), and any charges which encumber the title of the property and which are filed in the provincial land registry office (e.g., mortgages, liens, judgments, etc.). Another term for freehold is *fee simple*. Fee simple ownership of property is referred to as an "indefeasible" title. Most owners of condominiums acquire fee simple interest.

Leasehold Interest

In this example, the holder of the interest in land has the right to use the land for a fixed period of time, for example, 50 or 99 years. The owner of the property (landlord or lessor) signs an agreement with the owner of the leasehold interest (tenant or lessee) setting out various terms and conditions of the relationship.

The contract in relation to a condominium would set out such conditions as maintenance requirements, restrictions on use of the land, building construction requirements, and other matters. The leasehold interest can be bought and sold, but the leaseholder can only sell the right to use the land for the time that is remaining in the lease—subject, of course, to any conditions contained in the original lease.

Both freehold interest and leasehold interest can be left in your will as an asset of your estate or specifically bequeathed in your will.

Tip #72: Understand the Various Types of Joint Ownership

You may wish to have shared ownership in the property with one or more other persons. There are two main types of joint ownership: tenancy-in-common and joint tenancy.

Tenancy-in-Common

In this form of ownership, the tenants can hold unequal shares in the property. Each party owns an undivided share in the property and therefore is entitled to possession of the whole of the property. For example, there could be five people who are tenants-in-common, but four of them could each own 1/10 of the property and the fifth person could own 6/10 of the property.

If the holder of a tenancy-in-common wishes to sell or mortgage his interest in the property, that can be done. When a buyer cannot be found and the tenant-in-common wants to take his money out of the property, he can go to court, and, under a legal procedure called *partition*, request that the court order the property be sold and that it distribute the net proceeds of sale proportionately.

Tenancy-in-common does not carry an automatic right of survivorship as in joint tenancy. In other words, if one of the tenants-in-common dies, the interest does not go to the other tenants but goes to the estate of the deceased. If there is a will, the interest is distributed under the terms of the will. If the deceased person does not have a will, there is provincial legislation dealing with that type of situation, and the person's assets, which would include the tenancy interest, would be distributed to relatives according to the legislation.

There are various reasons why some people prefer tenancy-in-common over joint tenancy. For example, if you are purchasing property with people who are not relatives, you might not want them to automatically have your interest in the property in the event of your death. People might prefer a tenancy-in-common if they have been previously married and have children from a previous relationship; in this case, they might want to specify in their will that a certain portion of the estate goes to those children individually or collectively. The only way this can be dealt with is in a tenancy-in-common situation, because the interest would be deemed to be an asset of one's estate. Another reason as to why people may prefer a tenancy-in-common is that they are putting unequal amounts of money into the property, and a tenancy-in-common structure would reflect those different contributions in terms of the percentage interest in the property.

Written agreements are frequently signed by tenants-in-common, setting out the procedures if one of them wants out of the situation. This can be done by giving the others the first right of refusal on a proportional basis to buy out the interest, or there could be a clause requiring the consent of the other tenants-in-common in approving of a potential purchaser, or there could be a provision requiring a certain period of notice to the other tenants before the property is sold. Another case when tenancy-in-common might be preferable would be when one of the owners of the property wishes to have the personal independence to raise money for other, outside interests, for example, a business. The tenancy-in-common portion could be mortgaged without the consent of the other parties.

Joint Tenancy

This is a situation in which an owner has an undivided but equal share with all the other owners. No one person has a part of the property which can be said to belong to either party specifically, because all the property belongs to all of the owners. At the time of purchase of the property, all the people who are joint tenants will show up on the title of the property equally and each of the joint tenants has the rights in law to possession of the whole property. These are the essential conditions involved in joint tenancy, and if any of these conditions are not met, then the ownership is deemed to be a tenancy-in-common and not joint tenancy. The title of the property will list all the parties' names and will clearly state that they are joint tenants. If the title does not specifically state joint tenancy, the situation is generally deemed to be tenancy-in-common.

You can terminate your joint tenancy relationship by simply mortgaging or selling your interest to one of the other joint tenants or to another party. For example, if there are three joint tenants, you would be selling or mortgaging 1/3 of the property. The act of mortgaging or selling your interest immediately creates a tenancy-in-common in most cases.

One of the main features of a joint tenancy is the right of survivorship. This means that if one of the joint tenants dies, the other automatically and immediately receives the deceased person's share. In other words, the deceased person's share in the joint tenancy is not passed on as an asset of his estate to beneficiaries, whether or not a will exists. It is fairly common for a couple to hold the legal interest in the property by means of joint tenancy. Thus, you should consider tenancy-in-common if you do not want to have your interest go automatically to the other parties.

Tip #73: What You Need to Know About a Legal Contract

Five main elements have to be present in order for a contract to be valid. These are mutual agreement, legal capacity, exchange of consideration, intention to be bound, and compliance with the law.

Mutual Agreement

For a contract to be binding, there must be an offer and an acceptance. The terms and conditions of the bargain must be specific, complete, clear, and unambiguous. The parties to the contract must be sufficiently identifiable.

An offer may be withdrawn (revoked) any time before acceptance by the other party, as long as that revocation is transmitted, ideally in writing, to the other party. If the offer has already been accepted without condition and signed to that effect before receipt of the revocation, a binding contract has occurred.

Legal Capacity

The parties to a contract must have the capacity to enter into a legally binding contract; otherwise, the contract cannot be enforced. Each party to a contract:

- Must be an adult (i.e., over the "age of majority," which varies from province to province but is usually 19 years).

- Must not have impaired judgment (i.e., the party must understand the nature and quality of what is involved in signing the contract); if a person is impaired by drugs, alcohol, stroke, or mental infirmity (diminished capacity), that condition would invalidate the contract if it were proven.
- Must not be insane in medical and legal terms.
- Must be able to act with free will (i.e., is not under duress or threat or intimidation).

Exchange of Consideration

This concept means that something of value must be exchanged by the parties in order to bind the contract. Usually, money changes hands, but "consideration" could mean another house by exchange, something of value to the other party such as a service or product or other benefit, or a promise to do one thing in exchange for another.

Intention to Be Bound

The parties must have the intention of being bound by the agreement and its commitments, and must expect that it will be a bargain that could be enforced by the courts.

Compliance with the Law

A contract, to be enforceable, must be legal in its purpose and intent. The courts will not enforce a contract which is intended to, or has the effect of, breaching federal, provincial, or municipal legislation.

Tip #74: What to Look for in a Purchase and Sale Agreement

Most purchase and sale agreements come in standard formats, with standard clauses, and are drafted by the builder, the local real estate board, or commercial stationers. There are generally spaces throughout the agreement for additional, customized clauses to be added. A contract prepared by a builder has distinctly different clauses from those of a standard form for resale, and there are considerable differences in the standard contract clauses from one builder to another, and from one real estate board to another.

There is a high risk that the standard clauses, or additional ones that you may choose to insert, will not be comprehensive enough for your needs; you may not even understand them or the implications of them—and sign the agreement regardless. Also, it is possible some clauses could be unenforceable or ambiguous. That is why it is so important to have a lawyer review your offer to purchase *before* you sign it. Regrettably, relatively few people do this, because they either don't realize they should, perceive it to be an unnecessary or costly legal expense, could cause delay that could cause a purchase to be lost to someone else, or are naive or too trusting. It would be false economy to save on a legal consultation, as the costs to obtain a legal opinion are very reasonable relative to the risk involved in signing a bad contract.

Alternatively, rather than seeing a lawyer before submitting an offer to purchase, some people may wish to insert a condition that states the offer is "subject to approval as to form and contents by the purchaser's solicitor, such approval to be communicated to vendor within X days of acceptance, or to be deemed to be withheld."

There are many common clauses and features contained in the purchase and sale agreement, many of which vary from contract to contract according to various circumstances—whether one is purchasing a new or a resale condominium, etc. A brief overview follows of some of the common features of the agreement for purchase and sale.

Amount of Deposit

A deposit serves various purposes. It is a partial payment on the purchase price, a good-faith indication of seriousness, and an assurance of performance if all the conditions in the offer to purchase have been fulfilled. The deposit is generally 5% to 10% of the purchase price. If there were conditions in the offer, and these conditions were not met, then the purchaser would be entitled to receive the full amount of the deposit back. This is one reason why it is important to have conditions or "subject to" clauses in the offer to protect one's interests fully. Most agreements for purchase and sale have a provision that gives the vendor the option of keeping the deposit as "liquidated damages" in the event that the purchaser fails to complete the terms of the agreement, and pay the balance of money on the closing date.

When making a deposit, it is very important to be careful whom the funds are paid to. If you are purchasing through a private sale and no realtor is involved, never pay the funds directly to the vendor; pay them to your own lawyer in trust. If a realtor is involved, the funds can be paid to the realtor's trust account or your own lawyer's trust account as the situation dictates. If you are purchasing a new condominium from the builder, do not pay a deposit directly to the builder unless it is held in trust by the builder's lawyer. The money should go to your lawyer's trust account, or some other system should be set up for your protection ensuring that your funds cannot be used except under certain conditions as clearly set out in the agreement,

The risk is high in paying your money to a developer, because if the developer does not complete the project and goes into bankruptcy, you could lose all your money, and in practical terms could have great difficulty getting anything back. Though most provincial governments have brought in legislation dealing with new condominium projects to protect the public on the issue of deposits—as well as many other condominium risk areas—legislation provides only partial protection.

Another matter you have to consider is payment of interest. If you are paying a deposit, you want to ensure that interest at the appropriate rate or based on the appropriate formula is paid to your credit. In many cases, deposit monies can be tied up for many months, or in a condo presale situation for many years. These delays could represent considerable amounts of interest.

Conditions and Warranties

It is important to understand the distinction between conditions and warranties, as it is very critical to the wording that you would be using in the agreement. A *condition is* a requirement that is fundamental to the very existence of the offer. A breach of condition allows the buyer to get out of the contract and obtain the full amount of the deposit back. An inability to meet the condition set by a vendor permits the vendor to get out of the contract.

A *warranty is* a minor promise that does not go to the heart of the contract. If there is a breach of warranty, the purchaser cannot cancel but most complete the contract and sue for damages. Therefore if a particular requirement on your part is pivotal to your decision to purchase the condominium or not, it is important to *frame your requirement as a condition rather than as a warranty.* Both vendors and purchasers frequently insert conditions into the agreement, sometimes referred to as subject clauses. You can see why the services of an experienced real estate lawyer are important to protect your financial interests. Refer to the next tip for examples of these types of conditions.

Risk and Insurance

It is important that the parties agree to exactly when risk is going to pass from the vendor to the purchaser. In some cases the agreement will state that the risk will pass at the time that there is a firm, binding, unconditional purchase and sale agreement. In other cases, the contract states that the risk will pass on the completion date or the possession date. In any event, make sure that you have adequate insurance coverage taking effect as of and including the date that you assume the risk. The vendor should wait until after the risk date before terminating insurance.

Fixtures and Chattels

This is an area of potential dispute between the purchaser and vendor, unless it is sufficiently clarified. A *fixture* is technically something permanently affixed to the property; therefore, when the property is conveyed the fixtures are conveyed with it. A *chattel* is an object which is moveable; in other words, it is not permanently affixed. Common examples of chattels are clothes washer and dryer, refrigerator, stove, microwave, and drapes.

A problem can arise when there is a question of whether an item is a fixture or a chattel. For example, an expensive chandelier hanging from the dining-room ceiling, gold-plated bathroom fixtures or drapery racks, or television satellite dish on the roof might be questionable as to whether they are a fixture or a chattel. One of the key tests is whether an item was intended to be attached on a permanent basis to the property and therefore should be transferred with the property, or whether it was the intention of the vendor to remove these items and/or replace them with cheaper versions before closing the real estate transaction.

In general legal terms, if it is a fixture and it is not mentioned in the agreement, it is deemed to be included in the purchase price. On the other hand, if it is not a fixture and no reference is made to it in the agreement, then it would not be included in the purchase price. To eliminate misunderstanding, most agreements for purchase and sale have standard clauses built into them which state that all existing fixtures are included in the purchase price except those listed specifically in the agreement. In addition, a clause should list the chattels specifically included in the purchase price, and they should be clearly described.

Adjustment Date

This is the date that is used for calculating and adjusting such factors as taxes, maintenance fees, rentals, and other such matters. As of the adjustment date all expenses and benefits go to the purchaser. For example, if the maintenance fee has been paid for the month of March by the vendor and the purchaser takes over with an adjustment date as of the 15 of March, there will be an adjustment on the closing documents showing that the purchaser owes half the amount of the prepaid maintenance fee to the vendor for the month of March.

Completion Date

This is the date when all documentation is completed and filed in the appropriate registration and all monies are paid out. The normal custom is for all the closing funds to be paid to the purchaser's solicitor a few days prior to closing. As soon as all the documents have been filed in the land registry office and confirmation has been obtained that everything is in order, the purchaser's solicitor releases the funds to the vendor's solicitor. More discussion of the steps taken by both the solicitors relating to the closing date is covered later in this section. *Note:* The adjustment date and the completion date are frequently the same.

Possession Date

This is the date on which you are legally entitled to move into the premises. It is usually the same date as the adjustment and completion date. Sometimes the possession date is a day later in order for the vendor to be able to move out; in practical terms, though, many purchasers prefer the adjustment, completion, and possession dates to be the same, if it can be arranged. One of the reasons is that the risks of the purchaser take effect as of the completion date, and there is always a risk that the vendor could cause damage or create other problems in the premises if he remains there beyond the completion date. As soon as your solicitor has advised you that all the documents have been filed and money has changed hands, your realtor or lawyer arranges for you to receive the keys to the premises.

Merger

This is a legal principle to the effect that if the agreement for purchase and sale is to be "merged" into a deed or other document, the real contract between the parties is in the document filed with the land registry. To protect you, it should be stated in the agreement for purchase and sale that the "warranties, representations, promises, guarantees, and agreements shall survive the completion date." There are exceptions to the document of merger in cases of mistake or fraud—technical areas that require your lawyer's opinion—but it is important to understand the concept.

Commissions

At the end of most purchase and sale agreements there is a section setting out the amount of the commission charged, which the vendor confirms when accepting an offer. Occasionally this section states that if the purchaser fails to complete the agreement after all "subjects" (subject clauses) have been removed, and therefore the sale collapses, the realtor can keep the deposit as a form of compensation. Naturally, if you are the vendor, you will not be pleased with this. You could therefore make sure the purchase and sale agreement states that if the sale collapses, at the option of the vendor the deposit monies can be deemed liquidated damages and the full amount go to the vendor. A discussion of the various types of agreements for listing and selling real estate through a realtor, and related commissions, is discussed in the section on Selling Your Condo.

Tip #75: Ensure that Conditions of an Offer Are Clearly Stated

A previous point in this section discussed the differences between conditions and warranties. To protect their interests, vendors and purchasers frequently insert conditions into the agreement. These conditions are also referred to as subject clauses and should:

- Be precise, clear, and detailed.

- Have specific time allocated for conditions that have to be removed (e.g., within 2 to 30 days). It is preferable to put the precise date that a condition has been removed, rather than merely refer to the number of days involved.

- Have a clause that specifically says that the conditions are for the sole benefit of the vendor or purchaser, as the case may be, and that they can be waived at any time by the party requiring the condition. This is important because you may wish to remove a condition, even though it has not been fulfilled, in order to complete the contract.

Tip #76: Conditions for the Benefit of the Purchaser

Here is a sampling of some of the common subject clauses. There are many others that you or your lawyer may feel it appropriate to insert.

- Title is conveyed free and clear of any and all encumbrances or charges registered against the property on or before the closing date at the expense of the vendor, either from the proceeds of the sale or by solicitor's undertaking.

- Inspection of property being satisfactory to purchaser (as well as a spouse, relative, or friend—stipulate).

- Inspection of property being satisfactory to purchaser by house inspector/contractor selected by purchaser.

- Sale of purchaser's current property being made.

- Receipt and satisfactory review by purchaser (and/or purchaser's lawyer) of project documents, such as disclosure, declaration, articles, rules and regulations, financial statements, projected budget, last 12–24 months of condo corporation minutes to owners, the management contract, estoppel certificate, etc.

- Confirmation of mortgage financing.

- Approval of assumption of existing mortgage.

- Vendor take-back mortgage or builder's mortgage.

- Removal of existing tenancies (vacant possession) by completion date.

- Confirmation by the condominium corporation that the condominium unit being purchased will be able to be rented.

- Existing tenancies conforming to prevailing municipal bylaws.

- Interim occupancy payments being credited to purchase price.

- No urea formaldehyde foam insulation (UFFI) having ever been installed in the unit.

- Vendor's supplying a certificate of estoppel at the expense of the vendor within a certain number of days of the offer's acceptance.

- Vendor's warranty that no work orders or deficiency notices are outstanding against the property, or if there are, that they will be complied with at the vendor's expense before closing.

Tip #77: Conditions for the Benefit of the Vendor

Here is a sampling of some of the common subject clauses. There are many others that you or your lawyer may feel it appropriate to insert.

- Removal of all subject clauses by purchaser within 72 hours upon notice in writing by vendor of a backup bona fide offer.

- Confirmation of purchase of vendor-back mortgage through vendor's mortgage broker.

- Satisfactory confirmation of creditworthiness of purchaser for vendor-back mortgage.

- Issuance of building permit.

- Builder receiving confirmation of construction financing.

- Registration of a subdivision.

Tip #78: Know Your Legal Options to Get out of a Signed Contract

There are instances wherein either the vendor or the purchaser may wish to back out of the agreement. Some examples are discussed below.

Rescission

In many provinces of Canada and states in the United States there is a "cooling-off" or rescission period whereby the purchaser of a *new* condominium has a period of time (usually from 3 to 30 days) to back out of the contract by giving notice to the vendor in writing. The vendor is obliged to pay all the money back without penalty that the purchaser has placed on deposit. In cases where legislation does not give an automatic right to rescission, the documents which are a part of the condominium package may have a rescission period built in. If you do not have a statutory right to rescission and it is not part of the documents relating to the purchase of a new condominium, then you may want to make it a condition of your offer.

Specific Performance

If the vendor or purchaser refuses to go through with a purchase and sale agreement when there are no conditions attached to the agreement, the other party is entitled to go to court and request the court to order that the breaching party specifically perform the terms of the agreement (that is, complete the transaction).

Damages

If one party refuses to complete the agreement, instead of suing for specific performance of the terms of the agreement, the other party can sue for damages. Damages refer to the financial losses that are incurred because the other party fails to complete the bargain. In general terms, you have to prove damages to obtain compensation. For example, if a vendor refuses to complete a deal because he thinks he can make $50,000 more on the sale of the house—the prices having gone up considerably—and if in fact it can be shown that he did sell it for $50,000 more after refusing to go through with your signed commitment, then you could claim $50,000 damages. Your loss could be quantified, assuming that there were not other reasons that could explain the difference in price. Alternatively, if the purchaser fails to complete the agreement and the vendor can show that he was relying on those funds and therefore that the purchase he had planned failed to occur, and so on down the line with various back-to-back purchases and sales that were all relying on the first, there could be considerable damages for which the purchaser can be sued.

Conditional Contract

If the vendor or purchaser has preliminary conditions (subject clauses) built into the purchase and sale agreement, and those conditions cannot be met, it therefore blocks the deal at the outset, no valid binding contract exists, and neither party is liable to the other.

Void Contracts

A contract is void and unenforceable if the required elements that make up a contract are not present, or if the contract is prohibited by statute. These elements of a contract were discussed earlier in this section.

Voidable Contracts

If one of the parties has been induced into entering the contract on the basis of misrepresentation—whether innocent, negligent, or fraudulent—that party may be entitled to void the contract. If the misrepresentation was innocent, generally the contract can only be cancelled and any money returned, and no damages can be recovered in court. If there is negligent or fraudulent misrepresentation, however, not only can the contract be cancelled, but damages can also be recovered in court. For example, if the vendor was going to provide vendor-back financing and relied on representations of the purchaser concerning his creditworthiness and ability to pay, and prior to completion of the transaction, by doing a credit check and/or other investigation, the vendor finds out that the purchaser is a terrible credit risk, then that could be deemed to be negligent or fraudulent misrepresentation and the contract could be cancelled for that reason.

To give another example, if the purchaser finds out before completion that the representation of the vendor or the vendor's agent is grossly untrue (e.g., if the vendor has indicated that zoning has been approved for subdivision purposes, and investigation shows that no application has been made for subdivision purposes), then the purchaser could get out of the contract and sue to recover damages, if any can be proven.

These are just some illustrations of the types of factors that could impact on the validity or enforceability of the contract. You can see how competent legal advice from a skilled real estate lawyer is necessary to minimize potential problems.

Tip #79: Understanding Project Documents

Project documents are documents that are registered with the land registry office to create the condominium and to deal with the administration or "government" of the condominium community. There is different terminology for these documents, depending upon the province. The project documents are executed by the owner/developer of the land on which the condominium is to be built. Although the contents of the project documents can vary from province to province, they all generally include the following:

- A plan or survey showing the perimeter of the horizontal surface of the land and the perimeter of the buildings.

- Structural plans of the building.

- A specification of the boundaries of each unit by reference to the buildings.

- A diagram showing the shape and dimensions of each unit and the approximate location of each unit in relation to the other units and the buildings.

- A certificate of a surveyor that the buildings have been constructed in accordance with the structural plans and that the diagrams of the units are substantially accurate.

- A description of any interests relating to the land that are included in the property.

- A statement of intention that the land and interests relating to the land are to be governed by the Condominium Act.

- A statement of the consent of every person having a registered mortgage against the land and/or an interest relating to the land.

- A statement of the proportions of the common interests, expressed in percentages.

- A statement of the proportions in which the owners are to contribute to the common expenses, expressed in percentages allocated to each unit, and the proportions of the common elements to which each unit is entitled in the event of demolition or destruction.

- A specification of any parts of the common elements that are to be used by the owners of one or more designated units and not by all the other owners (exclusive-use common elements).

- A description of the system of assessment for maintenance and operating expenses.

- A statement of the fundamental rights and obligations of all parties involved.

- A specification of common expenses.

- A specification of duties of the corporation.

- A specification of any allocation of the obligations to repair and to maintain the units and common elements.

Obviously, the project documents are very important. In effect they are the constitution of each condominium corporation and are intended to be permanent in nature. In most provinces the project documents cannot be amended or changed in any fashion without the unanimous consent of the owners and mortgage holders.

Tip #80: Understanding the Condominium Corporation's Bylaws

Bylaws are created to assist the successful operation of the condominium project. They cover such matters as the use of common elements, the conduct of members of the condominium, and provisions for changes to the project and its rules. Basically, bylaws are intended to provide a basis for the control, administration, management, enjoyment, and use of the individual units, common property, facilities, and assets.

Bylaws can be amended or revised by a majority vote of the owners as outlined in the project documents. The term *bylaw* does not have the same meaning in every province. Some provinces set out, in their condominium legislation, specific bylaws that must be used; although these statutory bylaws can be amended by majority vote, any amendments have to be filed in the land registry office. Other provinces merely require in their condominium legislation that bylaws have to be established.

One example of a matter that could be contained in the bylaws is a limit on the number of residential condominium units that can be rented out by owners, the rationale being that tenants may not behave as responsibly as resident owners and that that could change the delicate mix of the condominium community. For example, there might be a provision that only 10% of the units may be rented out; if there are 50 units, that would mean a maximum of five units can be tenanted. Naturally, this could be an important consideration to you. If it was your intention, for instance, to rent out the unit while you travel for two years, or if you intended to rent it out for investment purposes, you would need to thoroughly check into the bylaws and the number of units that are currently being rented out, to see if the maximum has been reached. Alternatively, you may wish to look at another condominium development or, in the case of your travel plans, have a condition in the offer to purchase that the offer is subject to consent from the condominium corporation to allow you to lease out the unit for a period of two years.

Other areas typically covered by bylaw provisions are:

- The number, qualification, nomination, election, term of office, and remuneration of the directors.
- Matters relating to the meeting, quorum, and functions of the board of directors.
- The appointment, remuneration, functions, duties, and removal of agents, officers, and employees of the corporation, and the security, if any, to be given by them to it.
- The management of the property.
- The use and management of the assets of the corporation. The maintenance of the units and common elements.

- Duties of the corporation.
- Authorization of the borrowing of money to carry out the objects and duties of the corporation.
- The assessment and collection of contributions toward the common expenses.
- The general conduct of the affairs of the corporation.

Tip #81: Understanding the Condominium Corporation's Rules and Regulations

The condominium corporation is permitted to make such rules and regulations as it may consider necessary to effect the enjoyment, safety, and cleanliness of the common property, common facilities, or other assets of the condominium corporation. The rules and regulations are intended to govern the everyday rights and obligations of the unit owners, and can vary according to the special needs and desires of each project. Carefully review the rules and regulations and make sure that you can live with them. Some of the more common rules and regulations are as follows:

- No barbecues are permitted on any patios without permission.
- No articles may be stored in the basement, except where stipulated. All common areas such as walkways, stairways, hallways, and entranceways must not be obstructed, in order to allow proper entry and exit from the building.
- Under no circumstances may children play in the public stairways, elevators, halls, or entranceways. Children are to play in the designated playground area only.
- No articles may be hung from any windows or patios.
- No wagons, bicycles, or similar vehicles may be stored in any of the public areas.
- Owners are not permitted to make any noises which could interfere with the rights and enjoyment of other owners.
- Dogs and cats are not permitted at all. Other pets must be confined strictly to the owner's unit, and these other pets cannot annoy or disturb neighbours.

- Any complaint relating to the quality or nature of maintenance service is to be reported in writing to the management company.

- No owner is permitted to enclose a patio by means of a permanent structure, such as a solarium, without consent.

Tip #82: Understanding the Disclosure Statement

Many provinces have a requirement that any sale of a new condominium by the builder/developer is not binding on the purchaser unless he has received a copy of a current disclosure statement. The Condominium Act that governs this requirement states that it only applies for residential purposes, and that if the disclosure statement is misleading or deceptive in any material sense, the party who has relied on the statement is entitled to damages for any loss suffered because of it. The types of provisions commonly contained in a disclosure statement are as follows:

- The name and municipal address of the person making the statement and the property affected by the statement.

- A general description of the property or proposed property, including the types and number of buildings, units, recreational facilities, and other amenities, together with any conditions that apply to the provision of amenities.

- The proportion of units, existing or proposed, which the declarant or proposed declarant intends to market in blocks to investors.

- A brief narrative description of the significant features of the existing or proposed project documents, bylaws, and rules and regulations governing the use of common elements and units, and any contracts or releases that may be subject to termination or exploration pursuant to provincial legislation.

- A budget statement for the one-year period immediately following the registration of the project documents.

- If construction of amenities is not completed, a schedule of the proposed commencement and completion dates.

- Any other matters that are required to be disclosed under provincial legislation.

- The budget statement referred to above should set out:

    - The common expenses.

    - The proposed amount of each expense.

    - Particulars of the type, frequency, and level of the services to be provided.

    - The projected monthly common expense contribution for each type of unit.

    - A statement of the portion of the common expense to be paid into a reserve fund.

    - A statement of the assumed inflation factor.

    - A statement of any judgments against the corporation, the status of any pending lawsuits to which the corporation is a party, and the status of any pending lawsuits material to the property of which the person making the declaration has actual knowledge.

    - Any current or expected fees or charges to be paid by unit owners or any group of them, for use of the common elements or part thereof and other facilities related to the property.

    - Any services not included in the budget that the person making the declaration provides or intends to provide, or any expenses he pays that might reasonably be expected later to become a common expense, and the projected common expense contributable to each of those services or expenses for each type of unit.

    - The amounts in all reserve funds.

    - Any other matters that are required to be disclosed under provincial legislation.

Tip #83: Understanding the Condominium Corporation's Financials

As you are buying into a "corporation" that has its own financial expenses that are ongoing or anticipated, you need to understand what they consist of.

Operating Budget

If you are purchasing a new condominium, in some provinces it is required that the developer provide budget projections and details as outlined in the above point. If you are purchasing a resale condominium, you should ask for the current or projected operating budget.

Financial Statements

If you are purchasing a resale condominium, it is important to obtain copies of the most recent financial statements. Most financial statements are audited by a professionally qualified accountant and include the following: an accountant's comments, a statement of income and expenses, a balance sheet, and other documentation. Naturally, it is only as current as the most recent financial fiscal year-end, but it will give you a profile of the financial health of the condominium corporation. If you do not understand financial statements, you should have them reviewed by your lawyer or accountant, or on a consulting-fee basis by a condominium management company not involved with the project you are considering.

Estoppel Certificate

An estoppel certificate (or similar document, depending on the province) can be requested from the condominium corporation on application by the owner, the purchaser, or a purchaser's agent. It is deemed to be conclusive evidence of the accuracy of the facts outlined in it, and can be relied on by the purchaser. The following is an outline of the main facts confirmed by an estoppel certificate:

- The amount of the monthly maintenance charges paid by the owner that is applied to the condominium corporation's administrative expenses and contingency reserve fund.
- The manner in which the monthly maintenance fees are paid.
- The amount of money expended by the condominium corporation for the owner and not recovered by the owner.

- The amount, if any, by which the expenses of the condominium corporation for the current fiscal year are expected to exceed the expenses budgeted for the fiscal year.
- The amount of the contingency reserve fund.
- That there are no amendments to the bylaws or, if there are amendments, that those amendments have been filed.
- That no notices have been given for a unanimous or special resolution that has not been voted on, other than those stated in the certificate.
- That there are no legal proceedings pending against the corporation of which it is aware, other than those stated in the certificate.

Insurance Trust Agreement

This is the document that provides for the distribution of insurance proceeds once a claim is made.

Statement of Recreational Amenities

This document outlines all the recreational and other facilities that are or will be provided to the condominium corporation. The document sets out details as to whether they will be owned or leased, and whether or not charges will be assessed for use by the members of the condominium corporation, and what those charges are or will be.

Tip #84: Understanding Property Management

It is important for you to understand that you can influence the management contract your condominium corporation will undertake with a property management company. Why? It can save you and your neighbours money.

Management Contract

This is an agreement between the corporation and the company that manages the project on a daily basis. The management contract can vary considerably from one development to another. The services provided may include comprehensive ones such as operation, maintenance, and management. Under most provincial legislation, as soon as the majority of the units has been sold, the new buyers can cancel or modify the management agreement. This protects the public from a developer's signing a long-term management contract at an expensive price with an affiliated company before the units are put on the market.

Ground Lease

If you are purchasing a leasehold condominium, you will want to obtain a copy of the basic ground lease between the original landlord and the condominium corporation. This lease will set out all the terms and conditions of the relationship between the landlord (the lessor) and the tenant (the lessee).

Tip #85: Understanding the New Home Warranty Program Certificate

Most provinces have a New Home Warranty Program, although there are differences between the provinces in terms of coverage under the program. In some provinces, the program is mandatory by law whereas in others it is an optional program for builders.

It is important to contact the New Home Warranty Program in your province to get further information on the exact warranty coverage provided. (Refer to the Appendix for a list of contact website addresses in various provinces.) The overall program applies to condominiums, apartments, townhouses, and other forms of residential homes, but in any particular province there could be some restrictions on the type of condominium structure covered.

According to the terms of the New Home Warranty Program, it is the builder's responsibility to repair, without charge, defects in materials and/or workmanship, and structural problems. As stated, the coverage can vary from province to province. In addition, any remainder of the warranty coverage applying to the previous owner is generally extended to the subsequent buyers for a fixed period of time. Deposit funds are also protected up to a limit.

Prior to your taking possession of the condominium, under the program you will be asked to inspect the building and note any deficiencies on a checklist form, and the builder will note on the form if and when problems will be remedied. Once you sign a certificate of completion and possession, this is filed with the program and a New Home Warranty Program Certificate, with an identification number, is given to you. If a problem occurs after the signing, the homeowner notifies the builder; if the problem is not adequately addressed, the program officials attempt to mediate the matter and rectify the problem within the limits of the coverage.

It is the builder who pays for the program, but sometimes the builder passes on the cost for each individual unit to the purchaser or otherwise adds it into the purchase price.

Tip #86: The Ins and Outs of Hiring a Lawyer

Whether you are the buyer or the seller of a condominium, it is essential that you obtain a lawyer to represent your interests—a normal precaution with any real estate transaction, but particularly important when dealing with a condominium. As you will realize by the time you have completed reading this book, there are many potential legal pitfalls for the unwary in the realm of condominiums. The agreement for purchase and sale and related documents are complex. To most people, the purchase of a home is the largest investment of their life, and the agreement for purchase and sale is the most important legal contract they will ever sign.

When dealing with a condominium purchase or sale, it is important to select a lawyer who specializes in real estate law and is particularly familiar with condominium law. Laws are unique and constantly changing in this area, and expertise is therefore required. Because a lawyer who does a lot of condominium-related work has become familiar with the documentation, he or she will save you time and provide you with peace of mind.

There are a number of ways to select the right lawyer for your needs:

- Ask friends who have purchased a condominium about the lawyer they used, whether they were satisfied, and why.

- Contact the lawyer referral service in your community. Under this service, sponsored by the provincial law society or a provincial division of the Canadian Bar Association, you can consult with a lawyer for about half an hour for either a nominal fee (usually $10–$25) or no fee at all. Make sure you emphasize that you want a lawyer who specializes in real state—ideally, condominium real estate.

- Look in the Yellow Pages under "Lawyers" and check the box ads, which outline areas of expertise.

- Check the Internet for lawyers in your geographic area who practise real estate law.

- If you are obtaining a mortgage, speak to the lawyer who is preparing the mortgage documents on behalf of the lender. If the lawyer you choose is also preparing the mortgage documents, you could save on the duplication of some disbursement costs and negotiate a package price. Be careful, though, to avoid conflict; you want to make certain that the lawyer provides you with a full explanation of the mortgage terms and conditions that might affect your interests. Keep in mind that the mortgage is being prepared on behalf of the bank, but at your expense. If you have any concerns in this area, obtain a separate lawyer to do the non-mortgage legal work.

Once you have made contact with a lawyer over the phone, inquire about the areas of his real estate interest and expertise. Tell the lawyer that you are looking for a person with expertise in condominium law. If the lawyer cannot offer this, ask who he would recommend.

If you did not obtain the referral through the lawyer referral service, ask the lawyer over the phone what a half-hour initial consultation would cost. In many cases, it is free as a marketing goodwill gesture.

Have all your questions and concerns prepared in writing so that you don't forget any, and prioritize your questions in case you run out of time. If you wish to make an offer to purchase, bring your offer-to-purchase document with you, and the details about the new or resale condo you are considering. Ask about anticipated fee and disbursement costs. If you are not pleased with the outcome of the interview for any reason, select another lawyer.

Notary Public

You may have heard the term *notary public* and assumed it means the same as "lawyer." This is not necessarily so.

In most provinces, a lawyer is also automatically a notary public, but a notary public is not necessarily a lawyer. Make sure you know the difference. A notary public is not formally trained, qualified, or permitted by law to provide a legal opinion on any subject. He or she can only prepare the required transfer of title documentation, necessary affidavit material, and other related documentary material, and file the documents in the land registry office. In other words, the services provided are primarily technical and procedural. Thus, the buyer or seller of a condominium is advised to consult a lawyer. In matters relating to condominiums, you certainly want a legal opinion considering the potential risks and pitfalls. Also, if you encounter a problem before completion or afterwards relating to the sale, you already have a lawyer who can deal with it.

Note: In the province of Quebec, lawyers are referred to as "notaries" (non-courtroom lawyers) or "advocates" (courtroom lawyers). Therefore in Quebec you would use a notary for your condominium purchase or sale transaction.

In summary, make sure that you select a qualified lawyer and consult that lawyer before you commit yourself to any final agreement for purchase and sale.

Tip #87: Understanding the Services the Purchaser's Lawyer Provides

There are many services provided by your lawyer at various stages of a transaction; these stages include before the agreement is signed, after the agreement is signed, just before the transaction closes, on the closing day, and after the transaction closes. What follows is a partial summary of some of the matters discussed and services performed in a typical real estate transaction. Each situation will vary according to the complexity and the nature of the transaction.

Before the Agreement Is Signed

Discuss the contents of the offer to purchase with your lawyer. If there is a counter-offer from the vendor, make sure that you continue your communication with your lawyer before accepting the counter-offer, unless it is simply a matter of the purchase price. You should also:

- Discuss with your lawyer the ways in which you intend to finance your purchase.

- Confirm any and all legal fees and out-of-pocket disbursement costs you will have to pay.

- Ask your lawyer about all the other costs related to purchasing the condominium that you should be aware of. The most common expenses are shown in the Condo Purchase Expenses Checklist in the Appendix.

- Discuss matters such as your choice of closing date, inspection of the property before closing, and any requirements that you want the vendor to fulfill.

After the Agreement Is Signed

Once your lawyer has received a copy of the signed agreement, the process of thorough investigation is carried out, to make sure that all the terms of the contract are complied with and that you obtain clear title to the property without any problems. In other words, your lawyer will be going through a process of making sure that all your rights are protected and that you are getting what you contracted for. The types of areas that a lawyer will check include the following:

Title of property

An agreement for purchase and sale normally states that the vendor is going to provide title free and clear of all encumbrances. Therefore, your lawyer has to make sure that there are no claims or other filings against the property that could impair the title that you are purchasing. When searching the title, you will be able to find out the name of the registered owner, the legal description, the list of charges registered against the property, and other documents that are filed against the property in the case of condominiums. The types of charges that may be shown against the property would include the following (terminology may vary from province to province, but the concepts are the same):

- mortgage
- right to purchase (agreement for sale)
- restrictive covenant
- builder's lien (claim for money owing)
- easement
- right of way
- option to purchase
- certificate under provincial family relations act restricting any dealing with the property
- judgment
- caveat (formal notice that someone has an interest in the property and the nature of that interest)
- *Lis pendens* (an action pending relating to the property—e.g., foreclosure proceedings)

- lease or sub-lease, or option to lease
- mineral rights by the government
- condominium project documents
- condominium bylaws

In addition, your lawyer normally needs to review the following documents or issues:

- Survey certificate (shows property is located properly and not encroaching on neighbouring properties)
- Property taxes paid
- Outstanding utility accounts paid
- Zoning bylaws complied with
- Status of mortgages being assumed or discharged
- Ensuring financing will be sufficient and in place on closing
- Compliance with restrictions, warranties, conditions, and agreements
- Fixtures and chattels that are included in the purchase price
- Review of documents prepared by solicitor acting for seller (if applicable)
- Review, as appropriate, all documents required relating to condominium purchase: project documents, bylaws, rules and regulations, financial statements, disclosure statement, estoppel certificate, and other relevant documents
- Property insurance coverage obtained
- Review of mortgage being obtained or assumed

Just Before Closing the Transaction

Just prior to closing there are various steps that your lawyer will go through, including:

- Preparing documents relating to any sales tax for the chattels that you may be purchasing.

- Signing any mortgage documents necessary and making arrangements for funding to the lawyer's trust account from the mortgage proceeds on filing.

- Showing you a purchaser's statement of adjustments that gives the balance outstanding that you have to come up with before closing the transaction. You normally have to provide these funds to your lawyer two days beforehand.

- Receiving for forwarding any post-dated cheques required for the mortgage lender.

- Preparing all documents for filing in the land registry office on the closing date; if a different lawyer is involved in preparing the mortgage, that has to be coordinated for concurrent registration.

On the Closing Day

On the date of closing the transaction, your lawyer will perform various services, including:

- Checking on the search of title of the property to make sure that there are no last-minute claims or charges against the title.

- Releasing funds held in trust after receipt of mortgage proceeds from the lender, if applicable, and sending an amount to the vendor's lawyer based on the amount they are entitled to as outlined in the purchaser's statement of adjustments.

- Receiving a copy of the certificate of possession from the New Home Warranty Program, as applicable.

- Paying any monies required on the date of closing as outlined in the purchaser's statement of adjustments—e.g., sales tax on chattels being purchased, land transfer tax, as applicable, and balance of commission owing to the real estate company, paid from the proceeds of the purchase funds due to the vendor—and as outlined in the purchaser's statement of adjustments.

After Closing the Transaction

Once the purchase has been completed, your lawyer will confirm that fact to you, and you can make arrangements with the realtor to obtain the keys to your home, or your lawyer will arrange to get the keys for you. Your lawyer will also:

- Send you a reporting letter with all the field documents and all the other related documents attached for your records, including an account for fees and disbursements that have been taken from the funds that you provided your lawyer in trust prior to closing.

- Arrange to obtain and register the appropriate discharges of mortgages that were paid off from the funds you paid for the purchase, unless the vendor's solicitor is attending to this obligation.

- Ensure that all the vendor's promises have been satisfied.

There are numerous costs involved in purchasing new property, as shown in the Appendix in the Condo Purchase Expenses Checklist. As to legal fees, you should be able to calculate these accurately in advance by making inquiries of your lawyer about his fee schedule. Most lawyers charge a fee based on a percentage of the purchase price. In the case of condominiums, there is a higher charge generally because of the extra documentation and responsibility involved on the lawyer's part, due to the nature of a condominium transaction. Although fees can vary from place to place because of market competition and other factors, between ¾% and 1% of the purchase price is normal. This relates only to legal fees and not to disbursements, which can vary considerably, depending on the nature of your transaction.

Tip #88: Understanding the Services the Vendor's Lawyer Provides

If you are a vendor, it is important that you obtain a lawyer to represent your interests in the sale transaction. Whereas it is customary for the purchaser's lawyer to be paid a percentage of the purchase price, it is customary for the vendor's lawyer to be paid on an hourly basis for time actually expended. In view of the fact that condominium transactions are more complicated and therefore take longer, you can expect that they will be slightly more expensive than a house purchase. An hourly billing rate normally falls between $150 and $200 or more, depending on the location of the property and the lawyer's level of experience.

The lawyer acting for the vendor will perform a wide range of services, the extent of which depends on each transaction. Some of the services that will be performed at various stages are discussed below.

Before the Agreement Is Signed

Before you sign the agreement, you should have selected a lawyer to represent you, and discussed the contract with him to make sure you are protecting your interests and not incurring any additional expense or unnecessary frustration. If you are presented with a written offer, there are basically three options open to you:

- You can accept the offer in the form in which it is presented, by signing the offer. In this event there is a binding contract between you and the purchaser.

- You can alter the offer, by making changes that are more suitable to you and having the offer resubmitted to the purchaser. By making changes to the purchaser's offer, you are in effect rejecting the offer and countering with a new offer. The purchaser can either accept your changes or make further changes and return the agreement to you, which then constitutes a new offer.

- You can ignore the offer completely, if you feel that it is unrealistic or otherwise unsatisfactory to you.

After the Agreement Is Signed

Once the deal has been reached in writing between the vendor and the purchaser, the vendor's lawyer will request various documents from you (the vendor) in order to assist in completing the transaction. The type of material that you should obtain depends on the custom in your area and provincial jurisdiction. All the documents may not be easily obtained, but you should attempt to provide the following:

- Real estate tax bills.

- Hydro or other utility bills.

- Copies of insurance policies.

- A survey, if you have one available.

- A copy of the deed to your home, if you are in a province that has such a system.

- A copy of any outstanding mortgages, with the address of the mortgage company, and if possible the mortgage account number and amortization schedule.

- If an existing tenancy is being assigned, details of the tenancy and any security deposits.

- Any condominium-related documents, such as project documents, bylaws, rules and regulations, estoppel certificate, and others that may be required.

- Last 24 months of minutes from the condominium council to owners.

Prior to completion of the transaction, you should make arrangements to notify the cable television and telephone companies that you want service disconnected from your address as of a certain date. Also, advise your insurance company to cancel the insurance policy on the day after the closing date.

Just Before Closing the Transaction

Your lawyer will prepare a deed or transfer document which you must sign before title can be passed to the purchaser. Your lawyer will also prepare the vendor's and the purchaser's statement of adjustments. In some provinces or regions, the custom is for the purchaser's lawyer to prepare the conveyancing (property transfer) documents for the vendor to sign and prepare the vendor's and the purchaser's statement of adjustments. These would then be forwarded for review to the vendor's solicitor and to the vendor before signing.

If a mortgage exists on your home, it is the responsibility of the vendor to discharge the mortgage in order that clear title to the property can be transferred. Your lawyer will obtain a copy of the mortgage statement showing the balance outstanding as of the closing date, and then "undertake" (legally promise) to the purchaser's lawyer that the mortgage would be paid off first from the proceeds of the purchase.

If you are a non-resident of Canada, a *withholding tax* will be kept back from the sale proceeds and remitted to the Canada Revenue Agency. This tax is remitted because a non-resident could be making a profit or capital gain on the sale of the property, and is required to pay tax on that property, but Revenue

Canada could have difficulty collecting from someone who is a non-resident. This problem is eliminated by having funds paid directly from the sale proceeds, and rationalized in the following year's tax return. How much should be held back varies with the circumstances. Your lawyer will advise you and find out the amount of the withholding tax.

On the Closing Day

On the date of closing, your lawyer or his agent will meet the purchaser's lawyer or his agent at the land registry office in order that the transfer documents can be filed, changing title.

After Closing the Transaction

After the transaction has been completed, and your lawyer has received the appropriate money based on the vendor's statement of adjustments, he will clear off any existing mortgages with those funds and have the mortgages discharged from the title of the property. You would then receive the balance of funds after the legal fees and disbursements have been deducted.

Finally, your lawyer will send you a reporting letter setting out the services that were performed and enclose any appropriate documents for your files.

Tip #89: Protecting Yourself with Home Insurance

You need to protect your condo investment by having adequate home insurance and avoid the pitfalls of having a claim denied. Here is a basic overview of terms and information that you should know to save money and grief.

Inflation Allowance

This coverage protects you against inflation by automatically increasing your amounts of insurance during the term of your policy, without increasing your premium. On renewal, the insurance company will automatically adjust your amounts of insurance to reflect the annual inflation rate. The premium you pay for your renewal will be based on those adjusted amounts of insurance.

Inflation allowance coverage will not fully protect you if you add onto your building or if you acquire additional personal property. This is why you should review your amounts of insurance every year to make sure that they are adequate.

Special Limits of Insurance

The contents of your dwelling are referred to as *personal property*. Some types of personal property insurance, such as jewellery, furs, and money, have "special limits of insurance." This means the insurer sets a maximum reimbursement amount for those types of property. If these limits are not sufficient for your needs, you can purchase additional insurance.

Your policy automatically includes some additional coverage to provide you with more complete protection. Each type of coverage included is listed under the heading "Additional Coverage."

Insured Perils

A peril is something negative that can happen, such as a fire or theft. Some policies protect you against only those perils that are listed in your policy. Other policies protect you against "all risks" (risk is another word for peril). This means you are protected against most perils.

Even if you have selected "all risks" coverage, you should not assume that everything is covered. It is important that you read the policy carefully in order to understand the types of losses that are not covered. For example, floods and earthquakes may not be covered if you live in a high-risk location for these types of perils.

Loss or Damage Not Insured

This is the "fine print," the sections that tell you what is not covered. The fine print is also known as *exclusions*, and all insurance policies have exclusions. Exclusions are necessary to make sure that the insurance company does not pay for the types of losses that are inevitable (e.g., wear and tear), uninsurable (e.g., losses due to war), or for which other specific policy forms are available to provide coverage (e.g., automobiles).

Basis of Claim Settlement

This section describes how the insurer will settle your loss. It's the real test of the value of your policy and the reason why you purchased insurance.

Replacement cost

You should purchase replacement cost coverage for your property. This is particularly important for your personal property (i.e., the contents of your dwelling and personal effects). Otherwise, the basis of settlement will be "actual cash value," which means that depreciation is applied to the damaged property when establishing the values. You therefore would get less money, possibly considerably less.

"New for old" coverage is available. All you have to do is ask for "replacement cost coverage" and then make sure that your amounts of insurance are sufficient to replace your property at today's prices.

Guaranteed replacement cost

This is one of the most important types of coverage available to a homeowner. You can qualify for this coverage by insuring your home to 100% of its full replacement value. If you do, then the insurance company will pay the full claim, even if it is more than the amount of insurance on the building. Make sure this is shown on your policy. Note that guaranteed replacement cost coverage applies only to your building and not your personal property.

There is usually an important exclusion. Many insurance companies won't pay more than the amount of insurance if the reason the claim exceeds that amount is the result of any law regulating the construction of buildings. Check this out.

Deductible

There is a deductible and the amount is shown on the Coverage Summary Page of your policy. It means you pay that amount for most claims (e.g., $250 or $500). The insurance company pays the rest.

As you can imagine, the cost to investigate and settle a claim can be considerable, often out of proportion when the size of the claim is relatively small. These expenses are reflected in the premiums you pay. By using deductibles to eliminate small claims, the insurance company can save on expenses and therefore offer insurance at lower premiums.

Conditions

This is a very important part of your policy. It sets out the mutual rights and obligations of the insurer and the insured. This section governs how and when a policy may be cancelled, as well as your obligations after a loss has occurred.

Purchasing Adequate Amounts of Insurance

Purchasing adequate amounts of insurance that reflect the full replacement value of everything you own is without a doubt the single most important thing you can do to protect yourself. The risk is that insurance companies will not pay more than the amounts of insurance you have purchased, so it is up to you to make sure the coverage is adequate and realistic. Review your policy annually.

Establish how much it would cost to rebuild the condo. This is the amount for which you should insure the condo, in order to make sure that you are fully protected. The condo corporation will have insurance to cover the whole condo development from a fire up to a certain amount. Obtain a copy of the insurance coverage and review the maximum amount. Your own home insurance will cover any damages to your unit. However, you want to obtain insurance coverage on your own condo insurance policy that will cover any shortfall under the condo corporation insurance coverage, in the event of catastrophic damage to the condo development by fire, etc. Speak to a professional insurance broker.

If you put an addition onto the condo or carry out major renovations, you should recalculate the replacement value, as your current amount of insurance doesn't take this into consideration. Notify your insurance company representative. The inflation allowance feature of your policy does protect you against normal inflation, but is not sufficient to cover major changes.

Contents Coverage

If you are using the home personally, the following discussion relates to personal use. Your policy provides coverage for your contents. You should make sure that this amount is enough to replace all your possessions at today's prices. If the home is rented to a tenant, they are responsible to obtain tenants' insurance. You should make that a condition of any rental agreement.

If you have a claim, the insurance company will ask you to compile a complete list of everything that you have lost. Ideally, you should maintain an inventory of everything: furniture, appliances, clothes, and other possessions. Estimating what it would cost you to replace them is a good way to check if your amount of insurance is enough.

At the very least you should keep the receipts for all major purchases in a safe place. Another good idea is to take pictures of your contents, or make a video of everything by walking from room to room. In addition, most insurance companies will provide you with a checklist, so you can compile a list of your contents. This may seem like a chore right now, but it can really save time and aggravation if you do have a claim.

As you could lose your inventory or photographic evidence in a major loss, you should store your records away from your home. The best place is a safety deposit box. Whatever method you use, remember that you should update it periodically, ideally annually, to make sure that it remains accurate.

How Insurance Companies Calculate the Premium

The pricing of insurance is governed by a principle known as the "spread of risk." This means that the premiums paid by many people pay for the losses of the few. When more dollars in claims are paid out than are taken in as premiums, then the premium paid by everyone goes up.

The premium you pay therefore represents the amount of money needed by the insurance company to pay for all losses, plus their expenses in providing the service, plus a profit factor, divided by the number of policyholders.

The potential for loss assessment is based upon a number of risk factors. Most of these risk factors are based upon where you live. Here are the three most important ones:

Fire

Although theft losses occur more often, fire still accounts for most of the dollars insurance companies pay out in claims. The potential severity of a fire is therefore based upon a municipality's ability to respond to and put out a fire.

If you own property that has a fire hydrant nearby, your premium will be lower because the fire department will have access to a large water supply. Fires in hydrant-protected areas can be extinguished at an earlier stage than those in less well-protected areas.

If you own in an area without hydrants or even a fire department close by, the premium will be even higher.

Theft

Statistics show that theft is narrowing the gap with fire for dollars paid out. Generally speaking, there is a much higher number of break-ins in cities than in rural areas. Insurance companies track the loss experience caused by theft, by area, and this is reflected in the premium you pay.

Weather

If your geographic area has a history of severe weather storms, such as windstorms, snowstorms, hail, or flooding, or earthquakes, insurance companies obviously look at these risks as well.

Ways to Reduce Your Premiums

You should never reduce your insurance coverage in order to pay a lower premium. If you ever do have a claim, it could cost you a lot more than any amount you might save.

However, many people don't realize there are ways to reduce the premium payment significantly. Here are some ways to save money:

Take a Higher Deductible

What exactly do you want protection for? What you are really concerned with is the possibility of a catastrophe, or a total loss. If so, you can save money by increasing your deductible. By doing so, you save the insurance company the expense of investigating and settling small claims. That saving is passed back to you in the form of a reduced premium.

Use Discounts

Always ask what discounts are available and see if you are eligible. Generally, discounts recognize a lower category of risk. Listed below are the most common types of discounts available. They could range from 5 to 10% premium discount each. You could utilize several of them. However, most insurance companies have a cap on the aggregate amount of discounts not being more than about 50% of the base premium.

- Mortgage-free discount
- Loyalty discount (e.g., a customer for more than 3 years)
- Block Watch discount (e.g., your community is a member of Block Watch)
- Mature discount (over 50 years of age)
- Senior discount (over 60 or 65 years of age)
- New home up to 10 years old discount (with a depreciated premium discount for each year the house is older than new)
- Monitored fire and burglary alarm (through a central station)
- Local alarm discount (built into the home that will go off when motion or fire is detected)
- Multi-line discount (if you have different types of insurance products with the same insurance company or broker, e.g., house, boat, car, etc.)
- Claims-free discount (this is a discount you don't have to ask for. Most insurance companies will reduce your premium automatically if you have been claims free for three or more years.)

Personal Liability Protection

This is the part of the policy that protects you if you are sued. If someone injures himself on your property and sues you personally, and a court determines that you are responsible, your insurance company should defend you in court and pay all legal expenses and the amount up to the limit of the policy.

There are many types of personal liability that you could be exposed to. For example, someone might trip on a carpet in your condo and become seriously injured or paralyzed, or if you have a townhouse condo someone may slip on the stair leading up to your front door. If you accidentally spill hot coffee on a houseguest, leaving a scar on their face that requires plastic surgery, you could be liable.

The normal minimum amount is $1 million. However, you can increase this amount if you want. It is cheap money for peace of mind to obtain higher insurance for a "doomsday scenario." It is highly advised that you obtain enhanced coverage in addition to your personal liability protection. This extends and expands the protection beyond the current limits and maximum of your core homeowner policy. It might cost less than $100 annually to get $5 million coverage personally. Maybe for $100 you can get $10 million coverage. Your spouse or partner can also obtain enhanced personal coverage so both of you are protected. There has to be separately named coverage for each person, as both of you could, and most likely would, be sued in a doomsday scenario.

Here are some scary examples to show the benefits of enhanced personal liability protection. Say someone is paralyzed as a result of a fall in your home. Both you and your partner are sued and are found personally negligent and the award is $3 million. You are covered for only $1 million on your basic homeowner policy, leaving a $2 million shortfall. Or maybe you are driving a car while on vacation in the U.S., and accidentally hit someone who is a 50-year-old litigation lawyer or cardiac surgeon earning US$1 million a year. You have $1 million (Canadian funds) personal liability protection. The award is US$15 million. Fortunately, both you and your partner have a $10 million enhanced personal liability policy, with a combined $20 million of coverage for which you each paid $150 annually as a premium. This extended personal liability protection kicks in once your core policy coverage has been used up. So, in this hypothetical example, you did not have a shortfall (given the prevailing exchange rate), and can continue to financially live happily ever after.

There are specific exclusions that apply to this section of any policy, which are listed under the heading "Loss or Damage Not Insured." Make sure you read this carefully.

Home Office Insurance

If you are operating a part-time or full-time home-based business out of your condo, you need to obtain extra insurance coverage. This is normally done by means of an "endorsement" on your existing home insurance policy. From an insurance company policy perspective, if you are operating a business, then there is greater risk over strictly personal use. The extra policy premium is modest. The risk is that if you don't have this extra coverage and there is a claim that in some way relates to your home office use, the insurance company could deny coverage.

Tip #90: How to Avoid Being Sued

Every year, many people are injured while visiting the premises of others. The last thing you want is to be sued. The process is stressful, time-consuming, negative, protracted, and uncertain. Here are some suggestions to avoid problems. If you are renting to a tenant, your contract should cover hazard reduction and require the tenants to have tenant insurance coverage. As a condition of your tenancy agreement, request a copy of the policy.

Maintain Your Premises Well

Most injuries are caused by "slip and fall." They are usually the result of a lack of maintenance. In winter, you should clear ice and snow from all walkways accessing your condo, i.e., townhouse format, if it is not cleared by the condo corporation. Exterior steps should be kept in good repair and a handrail provided.

Inside your house, carpets should be secured to stairs and floors, and floors kept free of toys or objects that could trip a visitor.

Serve Alcohol Wisely

If you serve alcohol to guests, you could be found responsible, to some extent, for their subsequent actions. Some courts have gone to extraordinary lengths to assign responsibility to a host. Good judgment is required. In particular, never allow an intoxicated guest to drive a car.

Other Hazards

You are potentially responsible for everything that happens on your premises. For example, if you have a dog, you are responsible for the actions of the dog. The list is almost endless. If you are renting to a tenant, you want to pass on the responsibility and liability as much as possible to your tenant. As mentioned earlier, you want to make it a condition of tenancy that the tenant must obtain tenants' insurance prior to moving in, and that they must provide you with a copy of the policy within a certain time frame.

The good news is that most injuries can be avoided by using nothing more complicated than common sense. All you have to do is be alert to the potential hazards on your own premises.

Tip #91: Why You Need an Up-to-Date Will

Your will is the most important document you will ever sign. With very few exceptions, everybody should have a will. A will is the only legal document that can ensure that your assets will be distributed to your beneficiaries according to your wishes, instead of by a government formula, and in a timely manner and with effective estate planning to save on tax. Your will takes effect only after your death and is strictly confidential until that time.

If you own real estate, it is particularly important to have a current will. Due to the complexity of a will, you do not want to do it yourself. You need to use the services of a lawyer experienced in will preparation.

There are no estate taxes or succession duties in Canada, but estate planning can minimize the amount that is taxed in other ways. Part of estate planning also includes having a power of attorney and possibly a living will. For a more detailed discussion of estate and tax planning, refer to the latest edition of the book *The Canadian Guide to Will and Estate Planning* by Douglas Gray and John Budd. Also, refer to the website www.estateplanning.ca.

About one in four people dies suddenly, leaving no opportunity for tax or estate planning if such a plan was not already in place. It is estimated that only one in three adults has a will, which means that when the other 2/3 die, the government has to become involved. Some people just procrastinate by nature or have busy lives and simply do not put a priority on preparing a will. Others do not appreciate the full implications of dying without a will or even think about it. And some people simply resist the reality that they are mortal. Preparing a will and dealing with estate-planning issues certainly faces the issue of mortality in a direct way.

Of those who do have a will, many do not modify it based on changing circumstances, wishes, or needs. People first think of preparing a will when they marry, have children, fly for the first time without their children, or when they hear news of a sudden death of a friend or relative. Once they complete a will, they tend to forget about it. Not updating your will can be as bad as not having one and could cause your beneficiaries much grief, stress, time, and expense, and your estate a lot of unnecessary taxes. Your marital status may have changed, assets increased or decreased, or you may have started or ended a business, moved to a new province, or a new government tax or other legislation could be introduced that should prompt you to revisit your estate plan. Some people do their own wills, and make serious mistakes in the process.

Negative Implications If You Own Assets and Die Without a Will

If you don't have a will, or don't have a valid will, the outcome could be a legal and financial nightmare and an emotionally devastating ordeal for your loved ones. This is compounded greatly if you have a business. Not having a will at the time of death is called dying *intestate*. Under provincial legislation, the court will appoint an administrator. If no family member applies to act as administrator, the public trustee or official administrator is appointed. Your estate will be distributed in accordance with the legal formulas of your province, which are inflexible and many may not reflect either your personal wishes or the needs of your family or loved ones.

While the law attempts to be fair, it does not provide for special needs. A home or other assets could be sold under unfavourable market conditions in order to distribute the assets. Your heirs may pay taxes that might easily have been deferred or reduced. There may not be sufficient worth in the estate to pay the taxes. Your family could be left without money for an extended period, and your assets may be lost or destroyed. There may be a delay in the administration of your estate and added costs such as an administrator bond. This is similar to an insurance policy if the administrator makes a mistake.

If you die without a will appointing a guardian for your young children, and there is no surviving parent who has legal custody, provincial laws come into effect. The public trustee becomes the guardian and manager of the assets that your children are entitled to. The provincial child welfare services assume responsibility for their care, upbringing, education, and health. A relative or other person can apply to the court for guardianship, but what happens to your children is left to the court's discretion.

Other Documents to Consider

Living Will

A living will is designed for those who are concerned about their quality of life when they are near death. It is a written statement of your intentions to the people who are most likely to have control over your health care, such as your family and your doctor. The name of a living will can vary depending on the province, for example, representation agreement, advanced healthy care directive, health care proxy, etc. A copy of your living will should be easily obtainable, and you should discuss it with those family members close to you. Give a copy to your spouse and family doctor. You should also review your living will from time to time.

The purpose of a living will is to convey your wishes if there is no reasonable expectation of recovery from physical or mental disability. Such a will might request that you be allowed to die naturally, with dignity, and not be kept alive by "heroic medical measures." It could also cover health-related issues that you would not be able or willing to deal with during extreme illness, such as moving to a private or public nursing home or a palliative care facility, and could give authority to certain persons or family members to make those types of decisions on your behalf. In some Canadian provinces, a living will is merely an expression of your wishes and is not legally binding on your doctor or the hospital. Other provinces have officially endorsed the concept through legislation if your written instructions are correctly done. For further information, contact the Joint Centre for Bioethics, University of Toronto, through its website: www.utoronto.ca/jcb. Also check out www.estateplanning.ca.

Power of Attorney

Many lawyers recommend a power of attorney (PA), commonly referred to as an *enduring* PA, at the same time that they prepare a will. The purpose of a PA is to designate a person or a trust company to take over your affairs if you can no longer handle them due to illness or incapacitation, for example. Another reason is that you may be away for extended periods on personal or business matters. A power of attorney is important if you have substantial assets that require active management. You can grant a general PA over all your affairs, or a limited one specific to a certain task or time period. You can revoke the power of attorney at any time in writing. A PA is valid only in your province. You would need to have a separate PA if you own assets in the United States or elsewhere.

If you do not have a power of attorney and become incapacitated, an application has to be made to the court by the party who wishes permission to manage your affairs. This person would be called a committee. If another family member does not wish to perform this responsibility, a trust company can be appointed, with court approval. Committee duties include filing with the court a summary of assets, liabilities, and income sources, with a description of the person's needs and an outline of how the committee proposes to manage the accounts and/or structure the estate to serve those needs.

Personal Information Record

If you were to die suddenly, have a stroke, or be critically injured, would anyone have an accurate and current knowledge of your personal, business, and investment matters? For most people, the answer to that question is no. That is why you need to prepare one, and keep it updated annually and when any financial matters change. Your family, executor, and trustee will think of you fondly for having the foresight to make the administration of your estate so much easier. This personal information record is normally kept with your will, for example, in your safety deposit box, with an extra copy kept at home.

To obtain a copy of a personal information record template, go to the website www.estateplanning.ca.

Tip #92: Rely on a Lawyer to Prepare Your Will

In almost all cases, wills should be prepared by a lawyer who is familiar with wills because he or she is qualified to provide legal advice and is knowledgeable as to how to complete the legal work. Using legal services is cheap money for peace of mind.

Depending on the complexity of the estate, however, you may also need to enlist the expertise of other specialists, including a professionally qualified tax accountant or a financial planner.

The legal fee for preparing a basic will is very modest, ranging from $200 to $300 or more per person. If your financial affairs and estate are complex, this fee could be higher because of the additional time and expertise required. A *back-to-back* will is a reverse-duplicate will (usually one for each partner or spouse), and is generally prepared at a reduced price.

Key Reasons for Consulting a Lawyer

To reinforce the necessity of obtaining a legal consultation before completing or redoing a will, just look at some of the many reasons when legal advice is specifically required because of the complex legal issues and options involved:

- You own or plan to own real estate.

- You currently own or plan to own investment real estate with others.

- You own or plan to own foreign real estate on your own or jointly with others.

- You own or plan to own your own business.

- You own or plan to own a business with partners.

- You are separated from your spouse but not divorced.

- You are planning to separate from your spouse or partner.

- You are divorced and paying for support.

- You are living in, entering, or leaving a common-law relationship.

- You are in a blended-family relationship.

- Your estate is large and you need assistance with estate planning to reduce or eliminate taxes on your death.

- You anticipate being a beneficiary of a substantial inheritance.

- You have a history of emotional or mental problems such that someone could attack the validity of your will on the basis that you did not understand the implications of your actions.

- You want to have unbiased, professional advice rather than being influenced by or under duress from relatives.

- You want to live outside of Canada for extended periods of time, for example, retire and travel south in the winter. Your permanent residence at the time of your death has legal and tax implications. For more information, refer to my book *The Canadian Snowbird Guide: Everything You Need To Know about Living Part-Time in the USA and Mexico.* Also check out www.snowbird.ca.

- You have a will that was signed outside Canada or plan to have one.

- You want to forgive certain debts upon your death, or make arrangements for the repayment of debts to your estate should you die before the debt is paid.

- You want events to occur that are difficult to describe accurately, such as having a spouse have income or use of a home until he or she remarries or dies and at that time the balance goes elsewhere.

- You want to set up a trust for your family, business, or investment real estate.

- You want to donate money to a charitable organization.

- You want to make special arrangements to care for someone who is incapable of looking after himself or unable to apply sound financial judgment. For example, a child, an immature adolescent, a gambler, an alcoholic, a spendthrift, or someone with emotional, physical, or mental disabilities or who is ill.

- You wish to disinherit a spouse, relative, or child because of a serious estrangement or the fact that all your children are now independently wealthy and don't need your money.

- You have several children and you want to provide one specific child with the opportunity to buy, have an option to buy, or receive in the will a specific possession of your estate.

As you can see, there are many reasons to consult with a legal expert for a will that is customized for your needs.

Tip #93: The Importance of Estate Planning

Estate planning refers to the process of preserving and transferring your wealth in an effective manner. From a tax perspective, your estate objectives, including a properly drafted will, include minimizing and deferring taxes, and moving any tax burden to your heirs to be paid only upon future sale of the assets. There are techniques to attain the above objectives, including:

- Arranging for assets to be transferred to family members in a lower tax bracket.

- Establishing trusts for your children and/or spouse.

- Setting up estate freezes, generally for your children, which reduce the future tax they pay on assets of increased value such as a business.

- Making optimal use of the benefit of charitable donations, tax shelters, holding companies, or dividend tax credits.

- Taking advantage of gifting during your lifetime.

- Minimizing the risk of business creditors encroaching on personal estate assets.

- Having sufficient insurance to cover anticipated tax on death.

- Avoiding probate fees by having assets in joint names or with a designated beneficiary.

For further information, refer to the latest edition of my book, *The Canadian Guide to Will and Estate Planning*. Also, check out the website www.estateplanning.ca.

CHAPTER 6

Selling Your Condo

Tip #94: The Best Time to Sell

There are various factors that determine when you might sell your condo. Here are three that may govern your decision:

- Traditionally, the seasonal period of April through September is an optimal time period.
- When the real estate market cycle is in your favour.
- When your realtor provides you with stats and facts of the market conditions and sales and listings that confirm the optimal sales climate.

Tip #95: Hints on Preparing Your Condo for Sale

It is essential to make your property as attractive in appearance as possible, whether you are selling it yourself or through a real estate agent. The unit must evoke a positive feeling with the prospective buyer in order to obtain a quick sale and the highest price. Ask yourself objectively what you perceive a prospective buyer's first impression would be. If you feel you cannot be objective or want a second opinion, have a relative or friend look at your unit with a critical eye and ask them to be honest and tell you all the negative aspects they see, as well as the positive aspects.

Part of getting your home ready for sale means getting rid of unnecessary possessions that detract from a sale. Give yourself plenty of lead time to remove items before putting your home up for sale, in order to make the process more acceptable and less stressful. You may have to allocate three or four months of weekends before you have cleaned out the excess. Many people are packrats and have a mental block about letting go of possessions accumulated over time. They feel more comfortable about being surrounded by familiar items, no matter how unattractive, junky, or impractical. Of course, this statement does not apply to you! If you are having difficulty deciding whether to keep certain items, ask yourself if you have used the item over the past year. If so, consider keeping it as long as it is still usable. If not, ask yourself if it has any real value to you, or considerable sentimental value. If not, get rid of it by selling it at a garage sale or donating it to charity.

Another important step, once you have completed all the home improvement procedures, is to prepare a list of things about your house that you like, e.g., special or unique features such as a workshop or solarium, or a beautiful garden. Do a list of the key selling points about the house, in your view. For example, if you have repainted the house, inside or out, replaced the carpets or had new landscaping done, those are key points to make your home attractive to a prospective buyer. Finally, do a list of the main points that you like about the neighbourhood, such as convenient shopping, transportation, schools, parks, or playgrounds. In addition, such factors as a quiet neighbourhood, friendly and helpful neighbours, lots of babysitters nearby, and a community spirit are important points to note. If you are using a realtor, give this list to your agent.

The following points discuss the main internal and external factors that you should deal with, in the process of getting your home ready for the market. For more information, go www.homebuyer.ca.

The Unit's Interior

Keep Things Clean

Keep windows sparkling and clean, inside and outside. Clean all mirrors. Have drapes, carpets, and rugs cleaned and vacuumed. If the carpet is especially worn, consider replacing it. Your home will likely sell faster, although you may not recover your full cost. Keep front and back entrances clear, clean, and inviting. Clean up any corridors, halls, or walkways.

Make the Interior Decorating Attractive

Major decorating before selling may be neither necessary nor desirable because many buyers will probably prefer to select their own colour schemes. On the other hand, if the paint is old, dirty, or dull, you may wish to paint the key areas or all of the inside of the condo in a light, bright, natural colour, such as white or beige. Make sure it is washable latex paint. Lighter colours make the room appear larger and brighter. Neutral colours make the room more flexible for any type of furniture. A dingy closet or a badly marked wall can be made much more attractive with a good scrub, a touch of fresh paint, or a bright strip of wallpaper. Try to have a natural flow from room to room, rather than having rooms that are not uniform or complementary.

Unclutter the Premises

Keep untidiness to a minimum. Rooms can look comfortable and lived in without being untidy. Vacuum and dust thoroughly. Keep kitchen and bathroom counters uncluttered and gleaming, tables uncluttered and dirty dishes out of sight. Clean up books, magazines, newspapers, and clothes that might be lying around in a messy fashion. Store or sell excess furniture if it makes the room look cluttered and small with little floor space. Since you want to make the home look more spacious, and you want to make it easy for prospective buyers to imagine themselves in your space, remove items that are too personal, such as children's toy bins from living room, wall-to-wall sports trophies from family room, etc.

Clean the Closets

Make the best use of space. Show your closet and storage areas to their best advantage. Stack linen neatly, hang clothes carefully, and use garment bags and shoe racks. Crammed closets look small, but well-organized ones appear larger than they really are. Closet organizers would show how efficiently space could be utilized. Remove all "junk" from storage space and discard it, give it away, or sell it at a garage sale.

Make Kitchens and Bathrooms Inviting

The two most important rooms to many buyers are the kitchen and the bathroom. It is particularly important to make those areas appealing. Keep both rooms immaculately tidy and spotlessly clean. You want to create the impression that the home is easy to maintain.

Tidy the Garage

If you are living in a townhouse or bare land condo, you may have your own garage or carport. Keep your garage or carport neat and organized to show all the extra storage space. A garage can be a selling point, particularly if viewers are accustomed to the parking or storage problems associated with apartment living.

Make Necessary Repairs

You may be accustomed to a broken window catch, dripping tap, sticking or squeaky door, broken switch covers, and loose doorknobs, but potential buyers will notice and develop a negative impression. Therefore, fix everything that could be irritating from the buyer's viewpoint as described, and anything else, such as wobbly towel racks, loose mouldings, holes in window screens, and stuck windows. Walk around your home, inside and out, and make a list of small but necessary repairs.

Make the Environment as Peaceful as Possible

Keep noise to a minimum to let prospective buyers and real estate agents examine your home without distraction. Quiet music in the background might have a pleasant effect, but noisy children or TV or stereo sounds can annoy prospective buyers. Ideally, you should be away from the house, along with the children and pets, while your home is being shown by the realtor.

Provide a Comfortable Environment

Make sure the building is at a comfortable temperature; fresh and airy on hot summer days and warm during cold days. The right number of lights should be turned on after dark, and a crackling fire presents a homey feeling on a fall or winter evening, or even during the day. Consider replacing conventional light bulbs with "green" bulbs that provide a natural light in order to create a brighter feeling. (They also show that you believe in conservation.) Freshly cut flowers in various rooms such as the kitchen, living room, dining room, bathroom, and master bedroom would be inviting. Potted plants are attractive. The delicious smell of baking coming from the kitchen can be appealing and make one feel at home. Be cautious about cooking, though, as some cooking odours can be quite offensive and linger for a long time.

Keep Pets out of the Way

Buyers may not enjoy being welcomed by a cat or dog. Some people are allergic to animals and others don't like them. Many people could be turned off by knowing that various animals have resided in the home. Ideally, remove the pets from the home during the showing. Also remove cat litter boxes and use a deodorant spray to minimize any odour.

Remove Ashtrays and Odour of Smoke

Many people do not smoke and are allergic or otherwise negatively affected by the odour of cigarettes. The vast majority of the population does not smoke. Therefore, if any occupant of the condominium is a smoker, make sure you have all ashtrays removed, drapes dry-cleaned, and carpets shampooed. Also consider washing or painting the walls to attempt to remove any odour of smoke, which might discourage a prospective purchaser.

The Unit's Exterior

Maintain Your Landscaping

If you live in a townhouse or bare land condo, keep your lawn, shrubs, hedges, and garden tidy and trimmed. Sweep up the sidewalk and driveway. Attempt to have colourful flowers and/or hanging baskets to project a positive and warm feeling.

Consider Buying a Doormat

If you don't have a doormat or it is old, consider buying a new one.

Remove Junk

Store or remove any outdoor items that may create a "junkyard" image, such as old tires, cars, or broken fixtures or appliances.

Organize Outdoor Items

Arrange and organize items neatly, such as firewood, outdoor furniture, and play equipment.

Make Repairs

Paint or stain areas that require it and repair any broken fencing. Repair any broken windows or screens, and then wash them for a brighter appearance.

Consider Painting the Home

If you live in an apartment or townhouse condo, you don't have control over the exterior paint, but if you live in a bare land condo, you do have that option. It may not be necessary to paint the home, but do a touch-up and paint the trim. On the other hand, if the exterior is peeling badly or looks dull and dirty, it will negatively affect the sale of your home, both in price and speed of sale. Therefore, consider repainting.

Check the Front Door

One of the first items inspected by a buyer will be your front door. Make sure it looks attractive. Otherwise, consider replacing it. Get new brass house numbers or repaint the old numbers. This comment applies more to a bare land condo, of course.

* * *

The preceding hints are simply basic guidelines to remind you how important it is to set the correct mood and environment for a person to want to buy your property. As mentioned earlier, the best approach is to try to see your property through the eyes of a prospective buyer.

Tip #96: Know the Pitfalls of Sale by Owner

You may be tempted to sell the property yourself. There is only one reason for doing so, and that is saving on a real estate commission. You may indeed save money. On the other hand, the saving could be an illusion. The only other motivation could be a personal challenge or learning experience, but the desire to save money is usually the main motivator.

Depending on the nature of the property, the market at the time, the specific realtor you are considering, and the real estate company involved, you can negotiate a reduced real estate commission. The problem with a reduced commission structure, though, is that if you want it listed on the Multiple Listing Service (MLS), other realtors will see the reduced commission involved, and may not be too inspired to spend time attempting to sell it when they can make a higher commission on other properties.

Here are some general disadvantages of selling a property yourself, as opposed to using a carefully selected and experienced realtor. The comments apply whether you are selling your principal residence or investment property. The following remarks are not intended to dissuade you from attempting to sell your own property, but to place the process in realistic perspective. In the end, you will have to balance the benefits and pitfalls and make up your own mind.

Inexperience

If you don't know all the steps involved, from the presale operation to completing the deal, you could and probably would make mistakes that could be costly to you. If you use a realtor who knows the market well in your community, you can capitalize on the correct decisions being made.

Selling Can Be An Emotional Roller Coaster

Many people, especially with a principal residence, tend to get emotionally involved in the sale process because of the direct interaction with the prospective purchasers. For example, frustration can be experienced due to rejection of the home, negative comments or fault-finding, people whose personality you don't like, or people who negotiate toughly on the price. These one-on-one direct encounters or comments can sometimes be taken personally, and therefore be a cause of stress.

If you use a realtor to act as an agent, you rarely (if ever) meet the prospective purchaser directly, either before the agreement of purchase and sale is signed, or before or after closing. This degree of anonymity reduces stress.

Time Commitment

You have to have open houses as well as show your property at times that may not necessarily be convenient to you. In addition, you are going to be spending time preparing the ad copy and staying at home to respond to telephone calls or people knocking on the door.

If you use a realtor, you will be able to save time by not having to be around when the property is shown or to answer phone calls. The realtor does all that for you, as inquiries go directly to the realtor.

Expense, Nature, and Content of Advertising

Costs include any daily or weekly newspaper classified and/or box ads, Internet, as well as a lawn sign. You would pay these yourself. In addition, you may not know what specific types of advertising would be appropriate for your type of property, how to write ad copy that would grab the attention of a reader and prospective purchaser, or how to identify and emphasize the key selling features of your property.

If you use a realtor, they pay for all the advertising costs. The nature and amount of advertising is negotiated at the time the listing agreement is signed. Not only could you get listed in the MLS book, which normally comes out weekly and is circulated to all member realtors, you could also be on the MLS internal realtor database, which is accessible to all realtors, on the Internet through the MLS website, and through the real estate company website if they have one.

Studies show that over 70% of homebuyers make their initial purchase short-list decisions by using the Internet. You could also be advertised in daily and/or community newspapers, and in special weekly real estate newspaper publications, which are available in most major cities. In addition, your realtor can show your property at a special realtor open house once the property is listed. All interested realtors therefore have an opportunity to personally view it. All the techniques described are various forms of advertising and marketing. An experienced realtor should also know how to write good ad copy and accentuate the key selling features of your property.

Limited Market Exposure

The previous point covered the comparative differences in market exposure in terms of advertising by yourself and the types of advertising a realtor could do for you. There is obviously a direct correlation between the nature and degree of market exposure and the end price. Clearly, self-advertising has limited exposure.

Potential Legal Problems

The prospective purchaser may supply you with his own agreement of purchase and sale. This contract may have clauses and other terms in it that could be legally risky, unenforceable, unfair, or otherwise not beneficial to you. You may not recognize these potential problems or risks. In addition, you could end up agreeing to take back a mortgage (vendor-back mortgage), when it would not be necessary or wise, or to accept a long-term option or other legal arrangement that could be risky.

If you use a realtor, the realtor should know and recognize what aspects of the agreement are unfair, unenforceable, or unclear, and advise you accordingly. The importance of having a real estate lawyer protect your interests before signing an agreement of purchase and sale is mentioned several times throughout this book. It is a cheap price for peace of mind.

Lack of Familiarity with Market

You may not have a clear idea of exactly what a similar property in your market is selling for, or the state of the real estate market at that point in time. This can place you at a distinct disadvantage. For example, if you are being unrealistic in your pricing, along with limited advertising exposure, you could literally price yourself out of the market. Prospective purchasers may not even look, let alone make an offer. You may eventually sell your property, but only after several price reductions and after a long period of time. Naturally, of course, this depends on the market and the nature of your property.

If you use a realtor, they should be familiar with the market in your area, especially if you select a realtor carefully who is experienced with your type of residential property, and knows your geographic area well. The pricing and overall marketing strategies recommended would therefore be customized for market conditions and general saleability.

Lack of Pre-screening of Prospective Purchasers

You would not generally know the art of pre-screening prospects in terms of questions to ask them over the phone. The end result is that you could waste your time dealing with people who are not, and never will be, serious prospects. You could also end up accepting an offer from someone who does not realistically have a chance of financing the house, or who asks for unrealistic time periods for removing purchaser conditions, which effectively would tie up your property during that time.

If you use a realtor, he can pre-screen the potential prospects over the phone or in person to limit a potential waste of time for you. When the offers are finally presented, you will have more serious prospects involved.

Offer Price Is Not Necessarily the Best

You may think the offer is the best offer from that prospective purchaser, or any purchaser, and therefore may accept it. That price may not be the best price at all. You may have started too low or too high for your initial asking price, based on emotion or needs (not reality); you may have received a "low-ball" offer from the purchaser that was never intended to be accepted but was designed to reduce your expectations; you may be inexperienced in applying real estate negotiating skills; or you may be subjected to effective closing skills on the part of the prospective purchaser.

If you use a realtor, the realtor should be able to eliminate all the above problems. The realtor would normally provide the following services: do the initial research and set the original asking price realistically and objectively, depending on the market conditions, nature, and condition of the property, etc.; know when a "low-ball" offer was received and that it was a tactical ploy, and attempt to find out the reasons for the offer, and whether the prospect was a serious one; suggest how to deal with offers in terms of counter-offers; know what negotiating skills to use in a given situation, and use them on your behalf; and know how to use effective closing skills.

Lack of Negotiating Skills

This problem was referred to in the previous point. You may lack adequate negotiating or sales skills, and as a consequence the price and terms you eventually settle for may not be as attractive as they otherwise could be.

If you use a realtor who is experienced and competent in selling your type of property in your area and who has a successful track record, you will benefit from that realtor's astute use of professional negotiating and sales skills. Another advantage is that the prospective purchaser will be dealing with your realtor, and you will probably never personally meet the purchaser before or after you accept the offer and the deal closes. Removing yourself from direct interaction with the prospective purchaser, and using an agent instead, enhances your negotiating position and the effective use of strategies.

Purchaser Wants Discount in Price Equal to Commission Saved

It is not uncommon for the prospective purchaser to determine what the fair market value is, and then ask to have an additional discount equal to the real estate commission you are saving. The primary reason why prospective purchasers are attracted to a "For Sale by Owner" is the prospect of getting a better deal than a property listed with a realtor, due to the commission otherwise built into the sale price. The primary reason why you are selling the property yourself is to save the full amount of any commission otherwise payable; hence the problem. A compromise may be possible whereby the asking price is reduced by 50% or 75% of the commission saved. Again, in practical terms, it is normally an illusion to think that you will save the full amount of the commission. The other related issue is if you save (say, $5,000) on a commission, after the purchaser saves an additional $5,000 on the purchase price (e.g., splitting the commission saving), would you not have a lingering doubt that you could have netted more if you had listed the house through a realtor and with MLS?

If you use a realtor, the above problem of course does not occur. There is a good chance you would have received more for your property. Statistically, if you had listed it and had greater market exposure, better pricing, and a realtor who had applied more experienced real estate negotiating and selling skills than you would have, a higher sale price would have been achieved.

Tough to Sell in a Buyer's Market

Buyers in this type of market are very price sensitive, negotiate toughly because they want the best deal, and have the time to be selective after comparing what is available in the market. You are at a disadvantage if you don't get all the exposure possible and use all the negotiating and selling skills available. You could wait a long time before finally selling, and the market could go down further by that time in a declining sale market (i.e., substantial supply of property but limited demand).

If you use a realtor, whether the market is a buyer's or seller's market, for the reasons outlined in this section, the statistical odds are that you would benefit in terms of your net sale proceeds.

*   *   *

The above summary of the key points shows that there are distinct benefits to consider selling through a realtor who is experienced and carefully selected. Of course, there are exceptions in certain situations where you may choose to sell, yourself, but you have to be very aware of the disadvantages and pitfalls. Most real estate investors realize the benefits of using a realtor and do so as a business decision, whether for buying or selling.

Tip #97: How to Find the Right Realtor

In chapter 4, how to select a realtor was covered in general. In selecting a realtor to sell your property, a proactive marketing program and proven sales track record in condo sales are key factors. Also, word-of-mouth reputation is very important, as is your confidence level.

Tip #98: Getting the Best Price

There are many factors that determine whether you obtain the optimal price for your condo in the market it is sold. Selecting a proactive realtor who is skilled at selling is critical. You can get a sense of the price level by looking at comparison sales in your building or area. To maximize the price, it is important that you have properly prepared your condo for sale (as outlined earlier in this chapter), to enhance the "emotional curb appeal" to a prospective purchaser.

Being realistic about your sales expectations is also important. Some people are emotionally attached to a certain price based on the sweat equity that was put into the home, or financial needs for the next home purchase, or retirement needs. None of these factors could bear any relationship to the realistic market price that a prospective owner would be prepared to pay in a competitive market.

Tip #99: Know the Contents of a Listing Agreement and Avoid Problems Post-Sale

The real estate listing agreement is usually a partially preprinted form with standard clauses and wording. The balance of the agreement is completed by the agent and the vendor, and covers the specific information with respect to the property being offered for sale and the nature of the contractual bargain between the agent and vendor. Because the listing agreement is a binding legal contract, you should be very cautious about signing it without fully understanding its implications or obtaining advice from your lawyer beforehand. The following section covers the general contents of, and the types of, listing agreements.

Contents of a Listing Agreement

A listing agreement performs two main functions. You are giving the real estate agent the authority to act on your behalf to find a purchaser for your property. The agreement sets out the terms and conditions of this agency relationship, including the commission rate or method of compensation for the agent's services, the length of time of the appointment (e.g., 60 to 90 days or more), when and how the fee or commission is earned, and how and when it will be paid to the agent.

Another feature of the listing agreement is the setting out of the details of the property being offered for sale. All pertinent details should be set out, including civic and legal address, list price, size of condominium, description of the type of condominium (e.g., apartment or townhouse), number and size of rooms, number of bedrooms, type of heating system, main recreational features, and other amenities of the development. Any chattels or extra features that are to be included in the list price should also be set out, such things as appliances, draperies and drapery track, and carpeting.

You should also insert other particulars in the listing agreement relating to the property for sale, including details of existing financing, the balance on the mortgage, the amount of monthly payments, and the due date on the mortgage. Any other mortgages should be listed as well. Annual property taxes should be set out, as well as any liens, rights of way, easements, or other charges on the property.

You should also include in the listing agreement specific details of the marketing that the realtor will be doing for you.

Once you have come to an agreement on all the terms and you are satisfied with them, the agreement will be signed and witnessed and you will receive a copy.

Tip #100: How Much Commission to Pay a Realtor

Real estate commissions are negotiable based on various factors, including the services provided. The traditional rule of thumb is 5% on the first $200,000 and 2.5% thereafter for an exclusive listing, and 7% on the first $200,000 and 2.5% thereafter for a multiple listing. (For definitions of these different types of listings, see the next tip.) However, you will find a considerable variance in commission rates due to the competitive marketplace. For example, all lawers do not charge the same fee for doing your mortgage documentation or tranfer of title.

Tip #101: Which Type of Listing Agreement Fits Your Needs?

There are three basic types of listing agreements that you may wish to consider when listing your property with a real estate agent: open, exclusive, and multiple listing.

Open Listing

In an open listing, the real estate agent does not have an exclusive right to find a purchaser for the property; you can sign any number of open listing agreements with as many different agents as you wish. Only the agent who sells the property earns a commission. But the problem with an open listing is that many realtors don't spend a great deal of time on the listing because of the lack of assurance that they will ever receive a commission on the sale of the property. This is because so many other realtors could also be looking for purchasers.

Open listings are more common in commercial sales than in residential sales, and in any event you should obtain legal advice on the drafting of an open listing agreement if you are considering such an option. To protect yourself, make sure that the agreement is in writing and the terms clearly spelled out.

Exclusive Listing

In this example, the vendor gives to the real estate agent an exclusive right to find a purchaser for the property. This right is given for a fixed period of time. The real estate agent is automatically entitled to receive a commission whether someone else sells the property, the vendor sells the property, or the property is sold at some future point to someone who was introduced to the property by the real estate agent during the listing period. An exclusive listing is normally for 30, 60, 90, or 120 days. In many ways, the shorter time period (e.g., 60 days), the more energetically the realtor will have to work, and the more options you will have to change your realtor if you are dissatisfied with the performance and service.

Multiple Listing

With a multiple listing, a realtor is given an exclusive listing, in effect, for a fixed period of time, but also the right to list the property with the multiple listing service (MLS). This system is computerized and is distributed to all members of the real estate boards who participate in the MLS. You will also be on the MLS website. In practical terms, this constitutes almost all real estate companies; the entire real estate network becomes like a group of sub-agents for the sale of your property. If some other agent finds a buyer, the selling company and the listing company split the commission. Multiple listings are generally for a minimum of 60 days.

Conclusion

Congratulations!

You have now finished exploring the 101 tips. You have demonstrated your determined resolve to expand your knowledge about the unique community-living experience called a condominium. You have also learned how to avoid the classic pitfalls.

You are now better informed than 99.9% of the condo-buying population! That gives you a huge competitive and insightful edge when making your condo purchase decision, whether you are buying for personal use or as an investment.

If you are interested in more information, please refer to the Reader Feedback section at the back of the book, or go to www.homebuyer.ca.

Thank you, and best of luck in finding a condominium that fits perfectly with your lifestyle and personal needs and wants.

Condo Buyer's Checklist

Contents

Indicate on the line provided your rating of the listed factor as: excellent, good, poor, available, not available, not applicable, etc.

A. General Information

Location of property:

- Condition of neighbourhood   _____
- Zoning of surrounding areas   _____
- Prospect for future increase in value   _____

Proximity of:

- Schools   _____
- Churches   _____
- Shopping   _____
- Recreation   _____
- Entertainment   _____

- Parks _____
- Children's playgrounds _____
- Public transportation _____
- Highways _____
- Hospital _____
- Police department _____
- Fire department _____
- Ambulance _____

Traffic density _____

Garbage removal _____

Sewage system _____

Quality of water _____

Taxes:

- Provincial _____
- Municipal _____

Maintenance fees/assessments _____

Easements _____

Quietness of:

- Neighbourhood _____
- Condo complex _____
- Individual unit _____

Percentage of units that are owner-occupied _____

If next to commercial centre, is access to residential section well controlled? _____

Is adjacent commercial development being planned? _____

Size of development related to your needs (small, medium, large) _____

Does project seem to be compatible with your lifestyle? _____

Style of development (adult-oriented, children, retirees, etc.) _____

Age of development (new, moderate, old) _____

B. Exterior and Common Elements

Privacy _____

Roadway (public street, private street, safety for children)   _____

Sidewalks (adequacy of drainage)   _____

Driveway (public, private, semi-private)   _____

Garage:

- Reserved space (one or two cars)   _____

- Automatic garage door   _____

- Security   _____

- Adequate visitor parking   _____

Construction material (brick, wood, stone)   _____

Siding (aluminum, other)   _____

Condition of paint   _____

Roof:

- Type of material   _____

- Age   _____

- Condition   _____

Balcony or patios:

- Location (view, etc.)   _____

- Privacy   _____

- Size   _____

- Open or enclosed   _____

Landscaping:

- Trees   _____

- Shrubbery, flowers   _____

- Lawns   _____

- Automatic sprinklers   _____

Condition and upkeep of exterior   _____

C. Interior and Common Elements

Intercom system   _____

Medical alert system   _____

Fire safety system (fire alarms, smoke detectors)   _____

Burglar alarm system   _____

General safety:

- TV surveillance   _____

- Controlled access   _____

Pre-wired for television and telephone cable   _____

Lobby:

- Cleanliness   _____

- Decor   _____

- Doorman   _____

Public corridors:

- Material used   _____

- Condition   _____

- Plaster (free of cracks, stains)   _____

- Decor   _____

Stairs:

- General accessibility   _____

- Number of stairwells   _____

Elevators   _____

Wheelchair accessibility   _____

Storage facilities:

- Location   _____

- Size   _____

Insulation:

(The R factor is the measure of heating and cooling efficiency. The higher the R factor, the more
efficient it is.)

- R-rating in walls (minimum of R-19; depends on geographic location)   _____

- R-rating in ceiling (minimum of R-30; depends on geographic location)   _____

- Heat pumps   _____

- Windows (insulated, storm, screen)   _____

Temperature controls:

- Individually controlled   _____

- Convenient location   _____

Plumbing:

- Functions well   _____
- Convenient fixtures   _____
- Quietness of plumbing   _____
- Suitable water pressure   _____

Heating and air conditioning (gas, electric, hot water, oil)   _____

Utility costs:

- Gas   _____
- Electric   _____
- Laundry facilities   _____

Soundproofing features   _____

D. Management

Condominium management company   _____

Owner-managed (condominium council/board of directors)   _____

Resident manager   _____

Management personnel:

- Front desk   _____
- Maintenance   _____
- Gardener   _____
- Trash removal   _____
- Snow removal   _____
- Security (number of guards, hours, location, patrol)   _____

E. Condominium Corporation

Activity of corporation   _____

Average age of other owners   _____

F. Recreation

Clubhouse   _____

Club membership fees (included, not included)　　　　　＿＿＿＿＿＿

Sports:

- Courts (tennis, squash, racquetball, handball, basketball)　＿＿＿＿＿＿
- Games room (ping pong, billiards)　　　　　　　　　　＿＿＿＿＿＿
- Exercise room　　　　　　　　　　　　　　　　　　　＿＿＿＿＿＿
- Bicycle path/jogging track　　　　　　　　　　　　　＿＿＿＿＿＿
- Organized sports and activities　　　　　　　　　　　＿＿＿＿＿＿

Children's playground:

- Location (accessibility)　　　　　　　　　　　　　　　＿＿＿＿＿＿
- Noise factor　　　　　　　　　　　　　　　　　　　　＿＿＿＿＿＿
- Organized sports and activities (supervised)　　　　　＿＿＿＿＿＿

Swimming pool:

- Location (outdoor, indoor)　　　　　　　　　　　　　＿＿＿＿＿＿
- Children's pool　　　　　　　　　　　　　　　　　　＿＿＿＿＿＿
- Noise factor　　　　　　　　　　　　　　　　　　　　＿＿＿＿＿＿

Visitors' accommodation　　　　　　　　　　　　　　　　＿＿＿＿＿＿

G. Individual Unit

Location in complex　　　　　　　　　　　　　　　　　　＿＿＿＿＿＿

Size of unit　　　　　　　　　　　　　　　　　　　　　＿＿＿＿＿＿

Are the floor plan and layout suitable?　　　　　　　　＿＿＿＿＿＿

Will your furnishings fit in?　　　　　　　　　　　　　＿＿＿＿＿＿

Is the unit exposed to the sunlight?　　　　　　　　　＿＿＿＿＿＿

Does the unit have a scenic view?　　　　　　　　　　＿＿＿＿＿＿

Is the unit in a quiet location (away from garbage unit, elevator

noise, playgrounds, etc.)?　　　　　　　　　　　　　　＿＿＿＿＿＿

Accessibility (stairs, elevators, fire exits)

Closets:

- Number　　　　　　　　　　　　　　　　　　　　　　＿＿＿＿＿＿
- Location　　　　　　　　　　　　　　　　　　　　　　＿＿＿＿＿＿

Carpet:

- Colour _____
- Quality/texture _____

Hardwood floors _____

Living room:

- Size/shape _____
- Windows/view _____
- Sunlight (morning, afternoon) _____
- Fireplace _____
- Privacy (from outside, from rest of condo) _____

Dining room:

- Size _____
- Accessibility to kitchen _____
- Windows/view _____

Den or family room:

- Size/shape _____
- Windows/view (morning or afternoon sunlight) _____
- Fireplace _____
- Privacy (from outside, from rest of condo) _____

Laundry room:

- Work space available _____
- Washer and dryer _____
- Size/capacity _____
- Warranty coverage _____

Kitchen:

- Size _____
- Eating facility (table, nook, no seating) _____
- Floors (linoleum, tile, wood) _____
- Exhaust system _____
- Countertop built in _____
- Countertop material (warranty coverage?) _____
- Workspace _____

- Kitchen cabinets (number, accessibility)   _____
- Cabinet material (warranty coverage?)   _____
- Sink (size, single, double)   _____
- Sink material   _____
- Built-in cutting boards   _____
- Oven (single, double, self-cleaning)   _____
- Gas or electric oven   _____
- Age of oven (warranty coverage?)   _____
- Microwave (size)   _____
- Age of microwave (warranty coverage?)   _____
- Refrigerator/freezer (size, capacity)   _____
- Refrigerator (frost-free, icemaker, single/double door)   _____
- Age of refrigerator (warranty coverage?)   _____
- Dishwasher (age; warranty coverage?)   _____
- Trash compactor/garbage disposal (warranty coverage?)   _____
- Pantry or storage area   _____

Number of bedrooms   _____

Master bedroom:

- Size/shape   _____
- Privacy (from outside, from rest of condo)   _____
- Closets/storage space   _____
- Fireplace   _____
- Floor and wall covering   _____

Master bathroom (en suite):

- Size   _____
- Bathtub   _____
- Whirlpool tub   _____
- Shower   _____
- Steam room   _____
- Vanity   _____
- Sink (single, double, integrated sink bowls)   _____
- Medicine cabinet   _____

Number of bathrooms   _____

Complete, or sink and toilet only?   _____

Overall condition of condo   _____

Overall appearance and decor of condo   _____

H. Legal and Financial Matters

Project documents (e.g., disclosure/declaration) received and read   _____

Bylaws received and read   _____

Rules and regulations received and read   _____

Financial statements received and read   _____

Estoppel certificate received and read   _____

Other documents (list): _____

_____

All above documentation (as applicable) reviewed by your lawyer   _____

Financial statements reviewed by your accountant or independent

condominium management company   _____

All assessments, maintenance fees, and taxes detailed   _____

Condominium corporation insurance coverage adequate   _____

Restrictions acceptable (e.g., pets, renting out unit, number of people living in

suite, children, etc.)   _____

Condominium unit insurance package estimate obtained   _____

All verbal promises or representations of sales representative agent, or broker   _____

written into the offer to purchase   _____

Other: _____

I. Overall Assessment

_____

_____

_____

Condo Purchase
Expense Checklist

In addition to the actual purchase price of your home, there are a number of other expenses to be paid on or prior to closing that you need to budget for. Not all of these expenses will necessarily be applicable.

Type of Expense	When Paid	Estimated Amount
Deposit	At time of offer	_____
Mortgage application fee	At time of application	_____
Property appraisal	At time of mortgage application	_____
Property inspection	At inspection	_____
Balance of purchase price	On closing	_____
Legal fees re property transfer	On closing	_____
Legal fees re mortgage preparation	On closing	_____
Legal disbursements re property transfer	On closing	_____
Legal disbursements re mortgage preparation	On closing	_____
Mortgage broker commission	On closing	_____
Property survey	On closing	_____
Property tax holdback (by mortgage company)	On closing	_____
Land transfer or deed tax (provincial)	On closing	_____
Property purchase tax (provincial)	On closing	_____
Property tax adjustment (local/municipal)	On closing	_____
Goods and Services Tax (federal)	On closing	_____

Type of Expense	When Paid	Estimated Amount
New Home Warranty Program fee	On closing	_____
Mortgage interest adjustment (by mortgage company)	On closing	_____
Provincial sales tax on chattels purchased from vendor	On closing	_____
Adjustments for fuel, taxes, etc.	On closing	_____
Mortgage lender insurance premium (CMHC or Genworth Financial)	On closing	_____
Condominium maintenance fee Adjustment	On closing	_____
Home and property insurance	On closing	_____
Life insurance premium on amount of outstanding mortgage	On closing	_____
Moving expenses	At time of move	_____
Utility connection charges	At time of move	_____
Home and garden implements	Shortly after purchase	_____
Redecorating and refurbishing costs	Shortly after purchase	_____
Immediate repair and maintenance costs	Shortly after purchase	_____
Other expenses (list):		
_____	_____	_____
_____	_____	_____

TOTAL CASH REQUIRED $ _____

Glossary

Administrators In Quebec, those persons the co-ownership has appointed to act as administrators of the immovables. Equivalent to *board of directors* or *condominium council.* The administrators are responsible to the co-proprietors and are entrusted with the conservation of the immovables and the maintenance and administration of the common portions.

Agreement of purchase and sale A written agreement between the developer and a condominium for purchase of a condominium unit; or, in the case of a resale, a written agreement between the condominium owner of a unit and purchaser. Also referred to as *purchase and sale agreement.*

Amenities Generally, those parts of the common property and its facilities that are intended to beautify the premises, and which are for the enjoyment of occupants rather than for utility.

Amortization period The actual number of years it will take to repay a mortgage loan in full. This can be well in excess of the loan's term. For example, mortgages often have 5-year terms but 25-year amortization periods.

Appraised value An estimate of the value of the property offered as security for a mortgage loan. This appraisal is done for mortgage-lending purposes, and may not reflect the market value of the property.

Assessment fee Also referred to as a *maintenance fee.* A monthly fee which condominium unit owners must pay, usually including management fees, costs of common-property upkeep, heating costs, garbage removal costs, the owner's contribution to the contingency reserve fund, and so on.

Assumption agreement A legal document signed by a homebuyer which requires the buyer to assume responsibility for the obligations of a mortgage made by a former owner.

Balance sheet A financial statement that indicates the financial status of a condominium corporation or project at a specific point in time by listing its assets, liabilities, and members' equity.

Blended payments Equal payments consisting of both a principal and an interest component, paid each month during the term of the mortgage. The principal portion increases each month, while the interest portion decreases, but the total monthly payment does not change.

Board of directors The directors of the condominium corporation formed under provincial legislation. Sometimes called just "the Board." In Quebec, the responsibilities of the "administrators" are generally the same as those for the board of directors in other provinces. Directors may have personal liability exposure.

Budget An annual estimate of the project's expenses and revenues needed to balance those expenses. There are *operating* budgets and *capital* budgets. (See also *Capital budget*.)

Buildings The buildings included in a property, usually referring to the parts which are divided into the units and the common elements.

Bylaws One of the documents used in the conferring of condominium status. Bylaws may be included in the condominium statute in some provinces. In other provinces, bylaws have to be created, but the words of the bylaws are not contained in the statute. Bylaws deal with the operational aspects of the condominium corporation and the duties and responsibilities of the board of directors. (See also *Statutory bylaws*).

Canada Mortgage and Housing Corporation (CMHC) The federal Crown corporation which administers the National Housing Act. CMHC services include providing housing information and assistance, financing, and insuring high-ratio home purchase loans for lenders.

Capital budget An estimate of costs to cover replacements and improvements, and the corresponding revenues needed to balance them, usually for a 12-month period. Different from an *operating budget* (see below).

Charge A document registered against a property, stating that someone has or believes he or she has a claim on the property.

Closing The actual completion of the transaction acknowledging satisfaction of all legal and financial obligations between buyer and seller, and acknowledging the deed or transfer of title and disbursement of funds to appropriate parties.

Closing costs The expenses over and above the purchase price of buying and selling real estate.

Closing date The date on which the sale of a property becomes final and the new owner takes possession.

CMHC See *Canada Mortgage and Housing Corporation.*

Collateral mortgage A loan backed up by a promissory note and the security of a mortgage on a property. The money borrowed may be used for the purchase of the property itself or for another purpose, such as home renovations or a vacation.

Common elements Those parts of the property that are owned in common by the unit owners (e.g., halls, elevators, parking area, swimming pool, etc.). In some provinces, they are referred to as *common property,* and in Quebec, as *common portions.* Under all provincial statutes, whatever the term used, it means all of the property except the units. (See also *Limited common elements.*)

Common expenses Expenses incurred by the condominium corporation in carrying out the duties and responsibilities as specified in the project documents, i.e., in the declaration.

Common funds Funds (such as a contingency/reserve fund) held by the corporation or administrators of the co-ownership of the immovables, but belonging to the unit owners.

Common interest The proportional interest in the common elements belonging to a unit owner. (See also *Unit proportion.*)

Common property See *Common elements.*

Condominium A housing unit to which the owner has title and in which the owner also owns a share in the common elements (such as elevators, hallways, swimming pool, land, etc.).

Condominium council The governing body of the condominium corporation, elected at the annual general meeting of the corporation. Similar to a *board of directors* (see above).

Condominium legislation The legislation enacted by the provinces and territories to permit both individual and shared ownership of portions of multi-unit developments. Describes what a condominium is, how one is created, and how it must be administered. Provinces may from time to time make significant changes to their legislation. For reliable guidance the reader should always refer to the most recent provincial legislation and seek the advice of a real estate lawyer.

Condominium management The firm or individual responsible for managing and maintaining the physical and financial administration aspects of a condominium. Hired by the board of directors.

Condominium plan In certain provinces, a plan which is registered and which in essence describes the total project and each of the units in it. (See also *Declaration* and *Description*.)

Contingency fund See *Reserve fund.*

Conventional mortgage A mortgage loan which does not exceed 75% of the appraised value or of the purchase price of the property, whichever is the lesser. Mortgages that exceed this limit must be insured by mortgage insurance, such as that provided by CMHC and Genworth Financial Canada. See *Fixed-rate mortgage.*

Conversion The changing of a structure from some other use such as a rental apartment to a condominium apartment.

Conveyancing The transfer of property, or title to property, from one party to another.

Co-operative A form of ownership in which the individual "owner" has a share in the co-operative, which body actually owns the property. The "owner" has the right to live in a housing unit by means of a lease but does not own the actual unit.

Co-proprietor In Quebec, a condominium unit owner. The actual form of ownership is called *co-ownership.*

Corporation The condominium association of unit owners incorporated under some provincial condominium legislation automatically at the time of registration of the project. It is called a strata corporation in British Columbia. Under each of the statutes it will differ from an ordinary corporation in many respects. The corporation, unlike a private business corporation, does not enjoy limited liability, and any judgment against the corporation for the payment of money is also a judgment against each owner. The objects of the corporation are to manage the property and any assets of the corporation, and its duties include effecting compliance by the owners with the requirements of the Act, the declaration, the bylaws, and the rules.

Declaration The document used in some provinces under the condominium legislation, and which, upon registration, submits the project to the provisions of the Act and creates the condominium. It is called a condominium plan in some provinces, and a strata plan in British Columbia. In Quebec it is known as the declaration of co-ownership.

Deed This document conveys the title of the property to the purchaser. Different terminology may be used in different provincial jurisdictions.

Description In some provinces, the document which is registered simultaneously with the declaration and which defines the total project and describes each unit. It sets out those parts of the condominium development that are to be privately owned, and those areas that are to be owned in common by the owners.

Destruction A legal concept. When a condominium project is seriously damaged, the owners must decide whether or not to rebuild it. If they decide the latter, the project undergoes destruction, is destroyed, a legal process which divides the condominium corporation's assets among its owners. In certain circumstances condominium owners can also "destroy" a corporation even if it has not been damaged.

Development The building or buildings and the land upon which they are situated. Sometimes used interchangeably with project (see below).

Disclosure statement A series of documents prepared by the developer and issued to proposed unit purchasers describing the property, and containing a budget statement for a set period immediately following the registration of the condominium. Until the purchaser receives a copy of the current disclosure statement, the agreement of purchase and sale can be voided by the purchaser in most provinces.

Down payment An initial amount of money (in the form of cash) put forward by the purchaser. Usually it represents the difference between the purchase price and the amount of the mortgage loan.

Encumbrance See *Charge.*

Equity The difference between the price for which a property could be sold and the total debts registered against it.

Escrow The holding of a deed or contract by a third party until fulfillment of certain stipulated conditions between the contracting parties.

Estate The title or interest one has in property such as real estate and personal property that can, if desired, be passed on to survivors at the time of one's death.

Estoppel certificate A written statement requested by the prospective purchaser of a resale unit. The estoppel outlines whether or not all maintenance fees and other payments to be made by the current unit owner are up to date. In addition, it outlines other important financial or legal considerations. Sometimes referred to as a *Status certificate.*

Exclusive portion In Quebec, the parts of the immovables owned by and reserved for the private use of the individual proprietor. (See also *Unit.*)

Fee simple A manner of owning land in one's own name and free of any conditions, limitations, or restrictions.

Financial statements Documents which show the financial status of the condominium corporation at a given point in time. Generally includes income and expense statement and balance sheet.

Fixed-rate mortgage This is the conventional mortgage that normally has a term of from 1 to 10 years, and amortized over 20 to 30 years.

Fiscal year The 12-month period in which financial affairs are calculated.

Floating-rate mortgage Another term for *variable-rate mortgage.*

Foreclosure A legal procedure whereby the lender obtains ownership of the property following default by the borrower.

Fraction In Quebec, an exclusive portion and a share of the common portions under the Civil Code. Each co-proprietor has an undivided right of ownership in the common portions. His or her share in the common portions is equal to the value of the exclusive portion of his or her fraction, in relation to the aggregate of the values of the exclusive portions.

GE Mortgage Insurance See *Genworth Financial Canada.*

Genworth Financial Canada A private insurer in Canada that insures high-ratio mortgages.

High-ratio mortgage A conventional mortgage loan which exceeds 75% of the appraised value or purchase price of the property. Such a mortgage must be insured by either CMHC or Genworth Financial Canada.

Immovables In Quebec, in reference to condominiums, all the land and buildings comprising the condominium project.

Lien A claim for the payment of money against a unit or a condominium corporation.

Limited common elements Those common elements whose use is restricted to one or more unit owners or, conversely, those which are not available for use by all unit owners. These areas are often referred to as *exclusive-use areas.*

Maintenance fees Fees for the upkeep of a project based on a unit owner's percentage share of operating and administrative costs of the condominium corporation. (See *Assessment fee.*)

Management agreement A contract between representatives of the condominium corporation and a management company to provide management services for the project's day-to-day operation, and also to provide overall administrative services.

Mortgagee The lender.

Mortgagor The borrower.

National Housing Act (NHA) Loan A mortgage loan which is insured by CMHC to certain maximums.

Offer to purchase The document which sets forth all the terms and conditions under which a purchaser offers to purchase his unit. This offer, when accepted by the seller, becomes a binding agreement of purchase and sale.

Operating budget An estimate of costs to operate the project and corresponding revenues needed to balance them, usually for a 12-month period. Different from a *capital budget* (see above).

Phantom mortgage A technique developers of new condo units may use to compensate for the legal requirement to pay interest on the purchaser's deposit toward the purchase price. Comes into operation once a unit purchaser enters into interim occupancy pending the registration of the condominium by the developer. Under the condominium legislation of some provinces, the developer can charge an "occupant rent," which consists of common expenses for the unit, an estimate of municipal taxes for the unit, and interest on any mortgage the purchaser is required to assume or provide under the terms of the agreement of purchase and sale.

A vendor (developer) take-back mortgage, payable on demand, is inserted in the agreement. The demand is normally made at the time of closing or within seven days; the mortgage is therefore "phantom." By inserting this provision, the developer obtains the right to charge interest on the balance of the purchase price, which could be more than the amount the developer has to pay the purchaser in interest on the deposit money. Since the legal enforceability of a given phantom mortgage might be questionable, legal advice should be obtained.

PI Principal and interest due on a mortgage.

PIT Principal, interest, and taxes due on a mortgage.

Principal The amount you actually borrowed, or the portion of it still owing on the original loan.

Project The entire parcel to be divided into units and common elements.

Project documents The documents required to create a condominium, including, where such are applicable in the provincial jurisdiction, the declaration, the plan, the description, and the bylaws.

Prospectus A written presentation prepared by the developer that outlines material facts about the offering to induce offers from prospective purchasers.

Purchase and sale agreement See *Agreement of purchase and sale.*

Rescission That period of time following the sale during which the buyer can change his or her mind, cancel the purchase agreement, and get a refund of funds paid on deposit. It varies from province to province from approximately 3 to 30 days.

Reserve fund A fund set up to cover major repair and replacement costs or other unforeseen expenditures. In many provinces a percentage of all monthly maintenance fees must be put toward the reserve fund, and it is non-refundable. A healthy fund should make special assessments unnecessary.

Rules and regulations Rules which the board adopts respecting the use of the common elements and units, to promote the safety and security of owners and property.

Schedule of interests upon destruction A schedule showing the proportionate amounts of the land and assets of a condominium corporation due to the individual strata lot owners upon the destruction of the corporation. (See *Destruction.*)

Special assessment An assessment above and beyond the monthly assessment, which the condominium council (for larger expenditures, generally 75% of the strata corporation members) may decide to levy for a special purpose, e.g., building a sauna or swimming pool. Primarily for unexpected or unbudgeted expenses.

Special resolution A resolution generally requiring approval of 75% of the condominium unit owners. Required for granting easements, acquiring or disposing of common property, or passing bylaws, etc.

Status certificate See *Estoppel certificate.*

Statutory bylaws Bylaws of the corporation set out as schedules to the Condominium Acts of various provinces. Automatically in force when the Act is invoked until repealed or amended by a new provincial statute.

Strata corporation In British Columbia, equivalent to the term *condominium corporation.*

Strata lot Term used in British Columbia to describe property subject to individual ownership. Similar to *unit* (see below).

Strata plan Term used in British Columbia. (See *Declaration* and *Description.*)

Title Generally, the evidence of right which a person has to the possession of property.

Undivided interest An individual condominium owner's partial interest in the project's common property that is not defined by boundaries but is an abstraction.

Unit In all provinces except British Columbia and Quebec, each part of the project subject to individual ownership. In Ontario this comprises not only the space enclosed by the unit boundaries, but all material parts of the land within the space at the time the declaration and description are registered. In British Columbia, called *strata lot,* and in Quebec, *exclusive portion.*

Unit entitlement The share of a condominium owner in the common property, common facilities, and other assets of the strata corporation.

Unit factor In some provinces, the share ownership in the common elements separate from the unit. The same factor also relates to voting rights and contribution towards common expenses. (See *Unit proportion.*)

Unit proportion Generally, the proportion of the total common expenses for which a condominium unit holder is responsible.

Variable-Rate Mortgage A mortgage in which the interest rate varies with the prime rate fixed by the mortgage company, which is in turn based on the prime rate of interest set by the Bank of Canada weekly. Generally is one or more percentage points lower than the conventional fixed-rate mortgage.

Vendor A person selling a piece of property.

Vendor take-back A procedure wherein the seller (vendor) of a property provides some or all of the mortgage financing in order to sell the property. Also referred to as *vendor financing*.

Helpful Websites

Here are some websites to assist you in your information and contacts research before buying a condominium.

General Information

Google Internet Search	www.google.ca
National Real Estate Institute Inc.	www.homebuyer.ca
Canadian Estate Planning Institute Inc.	www.estateplanning.ca
Canadian Enterprise Development Group Inc.	www.smallbiz.ca

Real Estate Listings

Multiple Listing Service	www.mls.ca

Housing Surveys and Stats

Royal LePage Survey of Canadian Houses Prices	www.royallepage.ca
Canadian Mortgage and Housing Corporation	www.cmhc.ca

Professional Associations

Appraisal Institute of Canada	www.aicanada.ca
Canadian Association of Home and Property Inspectors	www.cahpi.ca
Canadian Home Builders' Association	www.chbi.ca
The Royal Architectural Institute of Canada	www.raic.org
Canadian Bar Association	www.cba.org

Canadian Institute of Chartered Accountants	www.cica.ca
Certified General Accountants Association of Canada	www.cga-canada.org
Canadian Institute of Mortgage Brokers and Lenders	www.cimbl.ca
Canadian Real Estate Association	www.crea.ca
Financial Advisors Association of Canada	www.advocis.ca
Financial Planners Standards Council of Canada	www.cfp-ca.org
Insurance Brokers Association of Canada	www.ibac.ca
Canadian Life and Health Insurance Association	www.clhia.ca

Mortgage Insurance, Title Insurance, and Credit Reports

Canadian Mortgage and Housing Corporation	www.cmhc-schl.gc.ca
Genworth Financial Canada	www.genworth.ca
Equifax Canada	www.equifax.ca
First Canadian Title Insurance	www.firstcanadiantitle.com

Federal Government

Canadian Mortgage and Housing Corporation	www.cmhc-schl.gc.ca
Statistics Canada	www.statcan.ca
Bank of Canada	www.bankofcanada.ca
Canada Revenue Agency	www.cra-arc.gc.ca

Provincial Governments—Condominium legislation

Alberta	www.gov.ab.ca
British Columbia	www.fin.gov.bc.ca
Manitoba	www.gov.mb.ca/cca
New Brunswick	www.gov.nb.ca
Newfoundland and Labrador	www.gov.nf.ca
Northwest Territories	www.gov.nt.ca

Nova Scotia	www.gov.ns.ca/snsmr
Nunavut	www.nunavut.com
Ontario	www.cbs.gov.on.ca
Prince Edward Island	www.gov.pe.ca
Saskatchewan	www.saskjustice.gov.sk.ca
Quebec	www.soquij.qc.ca
Yukon	www.gov.yk.ca

New Home Warranty Programs

Alberta New Home Warranty Program	www.anhwp.com
Association provinciale des constructeurs d'habitations du Québec	www.apchq.com
Atlantic New Home Warranty Program	www.ahwp.org
British Columbia Homeowner Protection Office	www.hpo.bc.ca
Manitoba New Home Warranty Program	www.mbnhwp.com
New Home Warranty of Saskatchewan	www.nhwp.org
Ontario New Home Warranty Program	www.newhome.on.ca

Private Warranty Programs

London Guarantee Insurance Company	www.londonguarantee.com
National Home Warranty Programs	www.nationalhomewarranty.com
Residential Warranty of Canada Inc.	www.reswar.com
Wylie-Crump Limited	www.wyliecrump.com

Condominium Associations

The Canadian Condominium Institute	www.cci.ca
Condominium Homeowners Association of B.C.	www.choa.bc.ca
Vancouver Island Strata Owners Association	www.visoa.bc.ca

Reader Feedback and Educational Resources

Your candid feedback and constructive suggestions for improvement in future editions of this book would be most welcome.

If you would like to provide feedback, have additional educational information, be on a mailing list for a free e-mail newsletter, or be kept informed about any upcoming seminars in your area relating to real estate in Canada, please refer to the website below. Thank you.

www.homebuyer.ca

About the Author

Douglas Gray, B.A., LL.B., formerly a practising real estate and business lawyer, has extensive experience in all aspects of real estate and mortgage financing. He has acted on behalf of buyers, sellers, developers, investors, lenders, borrowers, tenants, and landlords. He also has wide experience as a personal investor in real estate for over 30 years, as well as being a landlord of many properties.

He morphed from a legal career to being a consultant, columnist, speaker, and author of 22 best-selling books, some of which are published in up to nine foreign-language editions. He has written eight books on real estate. His book on buying, owning, and selling a condominium was originally published in 1989 and was the first Canadian book on the topic.

Douglas Gray is very familiar with the condominium lifestyle. He has owned a townhouse condominium for 14 years, and has been actively involved in the condominium management issues as past chairman of the legal committee. In his law practice, he was involved in condominium litigation and resolution of condominium disputes. As a condo owner, he has learned first-hand the joys and challenges of the condominium lifestyle.

He lives in Vancouver, British Columbia.

His website is www.homebuyer.ca.

NOTES